"If returning Veterans co̶ [obscured] them transition home from combat, it should be this one."

— Jason, Army Ranger, Afghanistan War Veteran

"Daniel did justice to all of us who didn't have a voice when we came home from Vietnam. If I had this book in 1969, I think my life would have turned out quite differently. God bless him."

— Steve, USMC Infantryman, Vietnam War Veteran

"I bought my husband this book because a friend told me about it and once he started reading it, he didn't put it down. He literally read the entire book in one afternoon. Words cannot express how it has changed him. I cannot recommend this book enough."

— Lisa, Wife of an Iraq War Veteran

"It's about time that there was a book written about combat PTSD and the transition to civilian life that is written BY a Combat Veteran with PTSD who has made the transition to civilian life. Most books are written by a psychiatrist who is just reciting what he learned in medical school. It's like a bunch of virgins teaching about sex. This book is the real deal."

— Mark, Combat Engineer, Iraq War Veteran.

"I've never seen my husband show any interest in books about PTSD or even talk about his time in Vietnam. This book is different. Daniel has found a way to get through to him like nobody else has. He has used some of the techniques in this book, and he's a changed man. Words cannot describe the transformation."

— Susan, Wife of a Vietnam Veteran

"Before I read Lessons Learned, I was a robot. Just going through the motions every day. My life had no emotion, I was dead inside. It helped me understand that I may have bad days, but I'll have more good ones. It helped me learn how to live a happier life. It has made me a better father, a more loving husband and the best person I know I can be."

— Tony, Green Beret with multiple tours
to Iraq and Afghanistan

I would like to dedicate this book to all of the brave
warriors that never made it back from combat.
Your bodies are back on your native soil, but your minds
are still on the streets of Baghdad, in Ia Drang Valley,
in the Chosin Reservoir and on the beaches of Normandy.
You have served your country bravely,
and I hope this book can help you find peace.

Welcome home.

INTRODUCTION

I would like to start off this intro by telling you what I am not – I am not a doctor, I am not a psychiatrist, I do not have any degrees in medicine, and you should not consider ANYTHING in this book to be medical advice.

Now that you know what I'm NOT, it's important that you know what I am:

I'm a former Combat Medic for the U.S. Army. I like cheap beer and dirty jokes. I prefer peace but am ready to fight if necessary. I was lower ranking and was never in a senior position. I didn't earn any fancy medals or tabs.

I'm just a normal Veteran. There isn't anything special about me, in fact there are a LOT of Veterans that have done much greater things than myself.

However, they don't have a voice.

I know how that feels because there was once a time when nobody would listen to me. Yet, it's funny how now I can say, "I'm Daniel Hutchison, Author of Nowhere to Turn, and I've been featured on The Daily Show with Jon Stewart and The New York Times" and people look at me like I'm a big shot.

I can tell you one thing – I didn't feel like a big shot in 2009 when I almost took my own life. I didn't feel like a big shot when the VA turned me away. I didn't feel like a big shot when none of the politicians I wrote to responded to me. I didn't feel like a big shot when I was curled up on my bathroom floor crying like a baby when I couldn't sleep because there were nightmares waiting for me.

This book is the most intimate thing I can give to you, it's the tips and techniques that took me from being suicidal to a man that now enjoys his life. This is what is missing from the transition process. It still amazes me how the military has programs on transition and PTSD that are managed by people that have never been overseas. It's mind-blowing!

I have confidence that this book will improve the quality of your life. I have seen these same techniques help hundreds of other Veterans. This isn't theoretical, this stuff works! These are all things that I have learned along the way to help cope with my transition and deal with my PTSD.

This book isn't politically correct. I'm sure there are some things in here that will offend some people, and I'm ok with that. I wrote this book in the hopes that I can help just ONE of my brothers or sisters. If I have to anger a thousand people along the way, then so be it.

This book is for the warrior who has served in combat. While it may be written through the eyes of a twenty-something year old male who was a medic in Baghdad, it will translate to any Veteran, of any war. If you were a female deployed to Afghanistan, there are techniques that you can use. If you were an Infantryman in Vietnam, there are techniques that will be helpful to you. If you were a cook in World War ll, there is information that can help you in this book.

IT TAKES ONE TO KNOW ONE

I've spent nearly the last 10 years of my life on a journey. The starting point was me sitting on my couch with a pistol in my mouth. At that point, it seemed like the only logical answer. It seemed it was the only way to stop the pain. Suicide looks like a coward's way out until you're the one contemplating it. If there was another choice you'd take it, but you've exhausted all options. You've already tried everything. You've given your best. You've reached the end of the tunnel, and now this is your only option.

Luckily that night, a series of events happened. They weren't events that changed my mind. I still decided I wanted to die, I just wanted it to be less messy so that when my family found me, they wouldn't be haunted by the sight of what a .40 hollow point can do to a man's skull. Somehow I misjudged the amount of pills that I thought would end my life and I didn't die, I just fell asleep.

I awoke the next morning to a card that pointed me in the direction of what is called a Vet Center. I'll describe those in a future chapter, but it gave me hope. It gave me a spark. It showed me that there was something to live for, but more importantly it gave me a new lease on life.

I left there thinking that I hadn't always been this depressed. That I was once a little boy that woke up happy and ready to take on the world. That I was once full of joy.

But somewhere along the way, that little boy died. He became a man, then became a Soldier. Through a series of events, he eventually got colder and colder. The joy wore off a little at a time until there was no joy left, just misery. Which led to me sitting on the couch with my pistol.

So, if a series of events could take a boy from the point of being happy and joyful to a man that is suicidal, couldn't there be a series of events that could reverse that process?

Couldn't there be a series of events, coping techniques, and exercises that make life more enjoyable?

Well there was good news and bad news when I looked into an answer for this question.

The good news is that yes, there are bunch of self-help books and seminars to do this.

The bad news is that a majority of them were ineffective, and NONE of them were guided towards PTSD for Combat Veterans. Furthermore, most of the books that were written about PTSD were written by psychiatrists who hadn't even served in the military. I was not happy about that at the time, but by working with returning Veterans I understand how powerful it is to be able to relate to someone's story. A male that has never been raped could use his degree in psychology to help a woman that had been raped, but he would never be able to TRULY understand what she had been through. So how effective would the treatment be?

There wasn't a one-stop shop for me to learn what I needed to be able to live a healthy life. I went to seminar after seminar and read book after book. I took bits and pieces from each one and applied it to my own life. I am now happy and everyday my quality of life improves. It's a process, but I am nowhere near where I used to be, not even close.

I once had a Major who went to bat for me. My Chain of Command had me pinned against the wall, I reached out for help from them, but they swept it under the rug. They were trying to strong arm me into a trigger that I knew wasn't healthy for me at the time. I was an E-4, I didn't have any power at all. I remember telling her about it and expected her to say something similar to "I'll look into it" or something like that, but she didn't.

She looked straight at me, took off her rank and said "I'll kick whoever's ass I need to, you just let me know. I've got your back."

She smiled and said "It takes one to know one".

She was referring to the fact that it takes a crazy person to know a crazy person.

This journey has taken me a lot of places in life, and I've done a lot of great things, but I have always remembered that day. What I took from that conversation is that when you are in a position of power, you not only have the ability, but you have the responsibility to do what is right. To stick up for those who do not have a voice.

I have dedicated my life to helping Veterans. I know what it's like to not have a voice. You probably know that quite well. But now that I'm an author and have been on TV a couple of times, everybody looks at me as though I'm superior to the Veteran next to me. I'm not, not even a little bit. In fact, there are waves of Soldiers that deserve more recognition than myself.

However, I do have power, that's just the way that it ended up.

This book is my way to fight for you and me, and all of the Veterans that do not have a voice. This is my way to make it so that you don't end up on YOUR couch with a pistol. It's so that I can share some of the things that I found during my journey that helped me. This is OUR book. This is OUR story.

This is me taking off my "rank", and telling you "I'll kick whoever's ass I need to, you just let me know. I've got your back."

It takes one to know one.

PTSD IS A PHYSICAL INJURY

If you have PTSD, you are injured, not hurt. Some of you will be taken back by that, but it's true. When I was in my darkest days, I thought I just needed to quit being a pussy, to toughen up, to numb the pain with alcohol until I recovered. I seriously thought I was hurt and not injured. But that's not the case. I'm not going to get too deep into neuroscience, but PTSD is a NORMAL reaction to being involved in an abnormal circumstance.

It's probably most closely associated with Veterans, but many civilians get PTSD from car crashes, witnessing murders, burglaries, rape and other traumatic events.

Here is Webster's definition of PTSD:

"A psychological reaction occurring after experiencing a highly stressing event (such as wartime combat, physical violence, or a natural disaster) that is usually characterized by depression, anxiety, flashbacks, recurrent nightmares, and avoidance of reminders of the event."

We are actually lucky that we are living in a time in which PTSD is recognized. Over the past twenty years, we have had leaps and bounds as far as research comes with understanding it. However, it hasn't been around for only twenty years. It's been around since the first human was on this earth. This is because it is a NORMAL reaction in your body. As far as Veterans are concerned, it was first coined PTSD in 1980, but we have seen it in every war that has ever been fought.

In the Civil War it was called "Soldier's Heart".

In the first World War it was called "Shell Shock".

In the second World War it was called "Battle Fatigue".

This NORMAL reaction in your body can be seen with an MRI machine. It's not you being weak. It's a physical injury.

Now let me explain. I was a Medic in the Army. If you were falling behind on a ruck march or complaining of cramping, I would tell you the same thing the Soldier beside you would tell you...

"Suck it up and quit being a pussy."

Why? Because it was probably all in your head. But let's say it wasn't, let's say you really were cramping up, or let's say you had blisters on your feet that popped. You know what I would say?

"Suck it up and quit being a pussy."

That's because those things are you being hurt. Those are things that you can push through. In the end, you will be a stronger person for embracing the pain and continuing while you were HURT.

But there isn't ANYBODY in their right mind that would look at a Soldier that just got his leg blown off by a grenade and tell him to suck it up. Nobody would tell him to drive on. We'd put a tourniquet on it, stabilize the wound and put them on a bird to get help. We would do that AS SOON AS POSSIBLE. Why the difference? Because we can see the injury. Because we know they are injured and aren't going to get better until they get help. We wouldn't hesitate for a second.

How about the injured Soldier? Would they try to push through? Would they say "Don't worry about it, I'll be fine"? Would they attempt to go months or years without treatment? No, they wouldn't.

But that's what I see an incredible amount of Veterans do. I see clearly INJURED people who think they are hurt trying to push through. They are INJURED, and they are slowly bleeding to death.

So if you are a Veteran with PTSD, I need you to understand the following:

1. You are INJURED, not hurt.
2. You will NEVER be the same again.
3. You can live a happy, healthy life with PTSD.
4. You are not alone. There is a brotherhood that supports you, including myself

YOU ARE NOT ALONE

While we have come a long way in not only understanding PTSD, but raising awareness that it's a normal reaction to an abnormal event, there is still a huge stigma surrounding it.

That's understandable as 100 years ago Soldiers were shot for what was then described as "Cowardice". Back then they didn't even know what PTSD was exactly. Well, I don't think that was entirely true. I think there was a lot of ignorance around PTSD as we can look back to Roman conflicts and see evidence of PTSD. We can actually even see evidence of PTSD which dates back to the Mahabharat war in 3139 B.C.

We can look back at Veterans of the Vietnam War and see ignorance surrounding the stigma of PTSD.

Hell, it didn't even EXIST (officially) until 1980 when it was entered into the DSM-III, which is essentially the bible of Psychiatry.

As I sit here typing this, I find myself struggling to provide more and more facts because it is imperative for you to understand the following:

YOU ARE NOT ALONE.

You are not different than the Spartan Warriors or the Civil War Soldiers. You are a human being that is composed of flesh and bones and a brain.

In 490 B.C., if a Spartan warrior was shot in his leg, he would bleed. Today, if you were shot in your leg, you would bleed.

In 1862, if you were a Civil War Soldier and you were hit with a grape shot, you would be injured. Today, if you were hit with a claymore mine or artillery round, you would be injured.

War is the same but it's different. The Spartan Warrior, the Civil War Soldier and you are the same person.

The difference is that they had to hide their wounds out of fear of humility and sometimes even death. Yes, PTSD is just as much a physical wound as a leg amputation. So back then, a Veteran who was having nightmares might be around another Veteran also having nightmares, but they would likely never talk about it out of fear.

If you are reading this book, then you are living in a time where PTSD is widely recognized. We are living in a time where there is a lot of research being done to understand it and come up with effective ways to treat it.

Did you know that nearly 1 in 5 Veterans have PTSD? You are not alone, and it's important for you to know that. You have an entire community that you can relate to and fall back on. Admitting and being vocal about having PTSD is one of the most powerful things you can do. You might have a Veteran friend who thinks he or she is nuts for having nightmares and feeling isolated. Just by being open about having PTSD, that might completely put him or her at ease and break down some of their barriers and encourage them to get treatment.

WEAK PEOPLE DO NOT HAVE PTSD.

I pray that I can let just one Veteran know that they are not alone. Hopefully I can reach a TON of you guys, but even if it is just one person that I can help, I would consider this book a win.

I stand WITH those of you that are strong enough to admit you have PTSD.

My name is Specialist Daniel Hutchison, former Combat Medic for the U.S. Army.

I am a Son.

I am a Brother.

I am an Uncle.

I am a Veteran with PTSD.

YOU WILL NEVER BE THE SAME

You need to know something. Something important…

YOU WILL NEVER BE THE SAME.

You will never go back to the person you were before you went to combat. It's impossible. I don't care what advancements are made in medicine, it's not going to happen. I don't care what happens in the world of psychology, there will never be a treatment that will take you back to the person you used to be.

There was a time in my life when if someone would have told me that, it would have shattered me. That was my quest, that's what I was searching for. I wanted to GET BETTER. I wanted to read a book, or go to a seminar, or talk to another Veteran and find the magic key that would take me back to the way I used to be.

Finding out that it is impossible would have shattered me. Why? Because if I can't go back to the way I used to be, doesn't that mean I'm always going to be a lesser person? By default, doesn't that mean I'm no good?

The answer is NO. Well, I guess the answer is that it's really up to you. Understand that you will never go back to the person that you used to be, but that's not a bad thing. It's very realistic that you could become someone MUCH GREATER. Your combat and life experiences give you such a solid foundation to begin a new life, a new persona. You are light years above most others as far as maturity goes. You have compassion that most people will never truly understand. The unconditional love that you shared with your brothers and sisters is something that most people have never felt or expressed to anyone. That love is something that you can share with your spouse, kids, family and your friends.

Use that knowledge as a foundation to become the type of person that you want to be. I know this is cliché, but you have likely heard the phrase "Today is the first day of the rest of your life." Well, today is the day you are reborn. Today is the day that you get to decide what type of person you want to become. Do you want to become the old, pissed off Veteran that's bitter towards everybody?

Another possibility could be to stand tall. To not be afraid of your physical and mental scars and to be the best version of you that you can be. To use the horrible things you experienced in combat to catapult you to be a better citizen. To be the type of person that people will look at with admiration and respect.

The qualities are already there. You're using more energy to suppress them than it would take to just be yourself.

Stand tall and be proud of who you are. You are a Combat Veteran.

IT'S NOT YOUR FAULT

This section is near to my heart and while much of this, I wish I was talking to you about in person. I really do wish that it wasn't words on paper that you were reading. I wish that I could grab a beer with you and tell you the following:

IF YOU HAVE PTSD, IT IS NOT YOUR FAULT!

Not even a little bit.

IT'S NOT YOUR FAULT!

You don't have a medical condition that makes you dream of dead Iraqis.

Your parents getting a divorce when you were young didn't cause you to avoid fireworks because they remind you of incoming mortar rounds.

The reason that you have PTSD is 100% because you were in combat. The reason your brain is physically changed is because you were exposed to something that most people will never see in their lives.

I can't stress this enough. If I were there with you right now and your response was something similar to…

"Man, I dunno, I think it might be because…"

I WOULD GRAB YOUR FUCKING HEAD

LOOK YOU IN THE EYES

And scream the following…

"IT'S NOT YOUR FUCKING FAULT!"

I say that because I didn't know ANY of the information in this book when I first got back. First, I didn't know that PTSD was a physical injury. Second, I was already a little fucked up from my childhood, to be honest.

I'm not going to put it all out there, but my father committed suicide when I was 13 years old. Then my mother turned to drugs, and I really had to fend for myself through my teenage years.

Understandably, I was struggling with thinking that since I was already a little fucked up from childhood, maybe that opened up the doorway for me to being weak and getting PTSD.

Regardless, we can fast forward, I finally got the courage to file a VA claim. I finally got it together to file for benefits so that I could get mental health help for my PTSD through the Veterans Administration. I put in my packet, waited many months until one day, I received that yellow envelope that holds the decision letter.

DENIED

They justified denying my PTSD because I had told them that my father died when I was younger and that there are still some times that I'm sad about that.

NO.

My father died when I was younger. At first I dealt with it in unhealthy ways, I then found healthy ways to deal with it and most of that is in the past. I mean yes, I still sometimes have emotions attached to it, but in no way is that the cause of my PTSD.

I don't get the taste of blood in my mouth when I hear someone yelling in Arabic because of it.

The muffled sounds of a police helicopter doesn't wake me up in a sweaty sleep because of my childhood.

My PTSD and my memories of combat are just a normal reaction to being put in an abnormal situation.

So don't try to play it off, and don't let anybody tell you that you are weak or that your PTSD is caused by something other than your service to your country. Because it isn't.

CHOOSE THE SUN

It's been a long journey that started with me sitting on my couch with a pistol in my mouth, to the person I am today. While I am by no means a person that hugs trees and pets puppies and sings kumbaya, I am a man that has passion for life.

I choose the sun.

I've read over 100 self-help books and have been to dozens of seminars. Most of the seminars AREN'T geared towards a Soldier with PTSD. So I had to pick and choose what applied to me and what didn't.

I forget the seminar or book that I learned it from, but there was an ideology that stood out to me. It related closely to me, and yet, at the same time it didn't even come close. It basically stated that we all have a choice to either stand in the shade and be cold, dark, and miserable, or we could take a couple of steps and stand in the sun where we would feel the warmth and see the light. That being happy or being sad was basically a choice. That at any point we could take the few steps in our mind and live in happiness.

So I would argue that having PTSD isn't that simple. You don't just think "Hey, I don't want the nightmares anymore. I'll just shift my thinking and I'll be a happy-go-lucky guy (or gal)."

I would argue that someone without PTSD does have the choice to take just a couple of steps and stand in the light.

I think maybe a more accurate depiction of a Veteran with PTSD would be to say that you are stuck in a dark room with no lights. Somewhere hidden in the room is the key to get out, but it's a very messy room with a bunch of heavy objects that need to be moved to find the key. Once you find the key, you can open the door and step outside into the sunlight. The key is 100% in there.

It won't be easy to find, but you can definitely do it. I know because I've accomplished that mission. Hell, I've even written this book that will make it easier for you to find the key.

I say easier but in no way is it easy. Maybe a more accurate way of saying it is that I've written a proverbial map. The darkness is still there. The room is still a mess. The objects are heavier than anything you've ever lifted in your life.

This isn't going to be easy. Not even a little bit. This will be one of the hardest things you have ever done in your life, but it's worth it.

You're tired of living in the dark. You're tired of not feeling any happiness. You're ready to make a change. If you weren't, you wouldn't be reading this book. Trust in not only me, but in the knowledge within this book. I've read tons and tons of useless information on psychology, and listened to a bunch of idiots with PHDs talk about how "This is the best way to address PTSD". I've taken the good, thrown away the bad, added in the hard lessons I've learned along the way, and it's all here in this book. It's not watered down, and at times it may not be something that you want to hear, but this is a message from me to you. This is me trying to help you in the only way that I know how.

Let's do this journey together. Let's choose the sun.

GET COMFORTABLE BEING UNCOMFORTABLE

This book isn't a magical answer that will automatically have you skipping down the sidewalk singing love songs. This book is me sharing with you what helped me come out of a very dark place. To be 100% honest with you, I'm still not completely out of it. I have my good days and my bad days, but I have a lot more good than bad.

Some of the exercises and ideas I present to you in this book are scary. I know, I've been there. It's scary to step outside of your comfort zone. It's scary to put yourself in a position that might trigger you. It's scary to put yourself out there and show people that you have emotions after having to be tough for so long.

I want you to know that it's ok to have a bad day. It's ok to have a couple of bad days. What isn't ok is to give up.

Earlier I had mentioned to "choose the sun". I think that fits perfectly on the journey that is becoming a civilian. First you need to hone your skills so that you can find the key and unlock the door. The sun may blind you at first and sometimes you may just peek out the door. Then sometimes you may spend 15 minutes in the sun and come back inside. There may be some days where you just don't want to be in the sun, but then you may get to the point where you feel comfortable standing in it every day.

It likely won't start off easily. I know from experience. I'm not a guy who's fresh out of college with a degree in Psychology and telling you some things I read in a textbook. The exercises and ideas in this book WILL help you. They are what have helped me get out of a dark place and what I have used to help hundreds of Veterans live happy, healthier lives.

But you have to put yourself out there, you have to try. It will be uncomfortable at first, but it will get easier the more you do it.

The idea of going to a fair where there are a bunch of people might seem terrifying at first. It did to me, but now I have no problem going anywhere with large crowds. It wasn't a switch that I flicked or a chapter in a book that I read that made that possible. It was me starting to go to the grocery store during the day when there were people in inside (as opposed to midnight when it was empty), then it was me going to a park that had some more people in it, but still wasn't crowded. I worked my way up. Sometimes I would have to leave. Hell, I remember one time I left a cart full of groceries right in the middle of an aisle. That was one of those bad days that come along with the good days. But the next day I got right back to it. I never gave up, because I knew there was sun on the other side.

It was definitely worth going through those trials and tribulations in order to get to a point where I can go to a large fair with massive crowds and ride the rides, play the games, see the shows, and eat all of the delicious food.

Get comfortable with being uncomfortable. You owe it to yourself to live a happy, healthy life.

BREAK THE CYCLE

What I'm about to tell you is going to be a pretty hard pill to swallow, but it is life changing. If you are a Veteran living with PTSD, you can diminish a majority of your flashbacks, episodes, etc., just by doing the following:

BREAK THE CYCLE.

Have you ever noticed how sometimes you can be having a relatively good day and one little thing can push it slightly in the wrong direction, and everything snowballs out of control from there?

You can't control your episodes or when you have flashbacks or intrusive thoughts, but you can control how you respond to them.

This may sound confusing, but let me give you an example of what would be a common occurrence for me circa 2009.

I would go to the store and I would hear someone yelling really loud in Arabic. I would start thinking "I wish this piece of shit would learn our language", I would then continue to let my emotions control me (sometimes to the point of triggering a flashback), but even if it didn't trigger, it would still make me pissed. I would then go out of my way to say something like "Learn to speak English, mother fucker". I would then storm out of the store, go home and drink, and think about how he reminded me of a casualty or how he was just like those assholes over there that would plant a bomb on the side of the road. I'd continue to drink and let myself get pissed off. I would do this until I went to bed.

Well, since I was thinking about bad stuff before I went to bed, what do you think I dreamt about? That's right, I'd have a nightmare and wake up in the middle of the night.

The next day I would be pissed off because I didn't get much sleep. I'd be irritable and angry. So I would go to the store to get beer.

I'd hear someone yelling really loud in Arabic....

So it would all start over again.

Once I learned to just break the cycle, my life improved SO much. I mean, it was life changing. I'm going to say this again - You can't control your flashbacks, but you can control how you react to them.

I'm going to use the words flashback and episodes interchangeably, but once you have a flashback, identify that you just had one. Don't be ashamed that you had one. Don't be apologetic. Just acknowledge that you had one, take a second to look around and regain your awareness, and go about your day.

This sounds like a hard task in the beginning and it is. It's hard because it's something that you aren't used to doing.

Let's replay how the store incident works out for me now.

I go to the store and I hear someone yelling in Arabic. I think to myself "They were given the gift of freedom. They went from a third world country to the best nation in the world. Really, you would think they would at least have the common decency to learn the language. But this is just one small experience of my day, and I'm not going to let it anger me. I came here to get mustard and that's what I'm going to do."

It's literally that easy, guys. I mean in the beginning it's difficult, but after a couple of times it gets really easy. Plus, once you realize the effect it has on your life and how it can shift your mindset, it almost becomes effortless.

BREAK THE CYCLE.

TRAIN AS YOU FIGHT

"You shit-birds better get an IV in that casualty and get him on the bird. You have 3 minutes before I make your life a living hell!"

I remember the cadre screaming that at me on a blazing hot night in San Antonio during Combat Medic School. It was their jobs to push our bodies and minds to the limit to prepare us for the stressors of combat. I remember leaving Fort Sam Houston with an incredible amount of confidence. I could call in a medevac from memory, I could start an IV in low light conditions with a Drill Sergeant yelling at me, I could apply a tourniquet in the dark with one hand. I was ready to treat casualties and do my duty as a Combat Medic.

Or so I thought. I remember my first casualty in Baghdad was a local Iraqi who was brought to our clinic. It was a non-combat related injury. There was some miscommunication between the interpreter but his head was basically bashed in. To this day, we think one of the T-walls he was putting up fell on him. Regardless, our squad practiced what we had rehearsed several times. The Officer yelled for one person to take vitals, one to do a head-to-toe assessment, etc. He then pointed at me and instructed me to do an IV.

No problem, I've done numerous ones to rehydrate hungover Soldiers in the barracks. I've done literally HUNDREDS in Combat Medic School under wild, stress-induced conditions.

This was just a guy laying on a stretcher. It should be easy. But it was different. This was something I hadn't trained for, this was a real human being whose life was in danger. Previously I thought that I had been pushed to the limit. That nothing could be more stressful than the hell that my Drill Sergeants put me through, but I was wrong. If we failed, Drill Sergeant wouldn't take us out back and make us do PT until we puked. If we failed, Drill Sergeant wouldn't just call us a piece of shit and make us try it again. If we failed, a human life would be lost. A father, a brother, a son would perish.

When that occurred to me, what I now know as psychogenic shock accompanied with auditory exclusion and tunnel vision kicked in. I didn't know that at the time. All I knew was that sounds were getting muffled, my vision was getting wacky, I felt cold, and it was hard to move my hands.

39

I missed the vein. Not only did I miss the vein, but I advanced the catheter and withdrew the needle. This is something that should only have been done if I had visual confirmation that I was in the vein by seeing the blood flash in the chamber. I won't continue to use a bunch of medical jargon, but this was a rookie mistake. This is something that if I would have seen someone doing this a day before, I would have ridiculed them for their incompetence.

However, it wasn't incompetence. It was my brain reacting in a normal manner. It was me operating from a state of psychogenic shock.

The guy was basically brain dead when he arrived to us. His head was smashed in and his eyes were non-reactive and several other signs pointed to the fact that he wasn't going to make it. Someone else got an IV started and we got him on a bird. He died at the next echelon of care.

I remember feeling humiliated leaving the clinic that day. I remember feeling like the worst medic in the world.

Shortly after that event, I was sent to a much smaller base and quickly after that, the troop surge of 2007 began. We received casualties nearly every day. Each one got easier to treat and near the end, I could run an IV on a casualty covered in blood, that was squirming around in pain, who was pleading with me to not let him die because he had children at home, while my Sergeant was telling me to hurry up because the Blackhawk was en route.

So what was the difference? The casualties during the end were definitely more intense, the casualties towards the end were more graphic as well (amputations, etc.).

The difference was that my brain was learning to deal with the stressors that my Drill Sergeants were not able to replicate during training. See, I think that this is one of the biggest misconceptions about military training.

YOU WILL NEVER BE PREPARED FOR COMBAT UNTIL YOU SEE COMBAT.

That IV you ran on a simulated casualty is good practice, but a real world casualty is completely different.

Scoring expert at the range is easy. Hitting a moving target that is shooting back is different.

I often think back and I wonder what my thought process would be if I would never have had a chance to redeem myself by treating additional casualties. What if the first IV stick that I missed was my only trauma casualty over there? Would I have spent the rest of my life thinking I was a failure, that I wasn't a real Combat Medic? What if I hadn't have read "On Combat" by Lt. Col. Dave Grossman and acquired a better understanding of how the human body reacts under combat stressors?

I say that because there is likely a chance that there is a Grunt who is reading this book who missed a shot that would have killed an approaching suicide bomber who ultimately ended up detonating and killing one or more of his friends.

There is likely a chance that there is someone reading this book who, under stress, called in the wrong grid coordinates and the mortar crew didn't eliminate the enemy in time.

There is likely a chance that there is someone reading this book that failed to apply the tourniquet correctly in the back of a HMMWV after a grenade explosion.

It's likely that you are blaming yourself. It's not your fault, it's the way the human body responds to being in combat or exposed to stressors.

Think about this -There have been MULTIPLE reports during home invasion robberies where the police never arrive because the homeowner dialed 9-1-1 on their cell phones, but they forgot to press send. There are numerous reports of a co-worker who has had a heart attack, but EMS services were delayed because their co-workers dialed 9-1-1, but forgot to press 9 to reach an outside line. These are all instances of seemingly easy tasks that become complicated when our bodies respond to stress.

Combat is a lot more intense than that. I'm not telling you to forgive yourself. I'm not telling you to come to terms with the fact that you messed up. I'm telling you that you DIDN'T mess up. I'm telling you that you operated to the best of your ability at the time. Your body physically changed during that stressful event.

You may be able to run a 7 minute mile. You should be proud of that. You trained your ass off. However, if you had to run that same mile with weights on your feet, you wouldn't be pissed off that it took you 10 minutes to run it. You would understand that something was different that made it impossible to operate at the level of your current training.

FORGIVE YOURSELF

You can't change the past.

It seems so simple when I type that. It also seems easy to say that. Well, now it does. That was a different story when I first got back. It seemed easy to think back on what I should have or could have done differently when I was over there. It seemed easy to blame myself for what I thought were unforgiveable failures.

"If only I had…"

But the truth is, you are just using extra effort to make yourself feel bad. You are literally going out of the way to put yourself through misery that is not necessary.

It's absolutely impossible to go back and change the past.

As you read through some of the other chapters in this book, I hope you are able to understand the "time you failed" wasn't a failure at all. It was likely you making a mountain of an ant hill. That the time you failed to properly do your job was because of your body physically changing due to the stressors it was exposed to, or that your friend who you tried to save couldn't have been saved even if there was a hospital five feet away.

I still know that with me saying that, it may be difficult to let go. I'm going to share with you a powerful exercise I learned a while ago.

Forgive yourself. Write a letter forgiving yourself and allowing you to be free. I once wrote a letter similar to:

Daniel,

I forgive you for not being able to save Sergeant Smith that day in June. I know you tried the best you could. I understand you were a 25 year old kid with 16 weeks of medical training and you were put in a very wild situation.

I unconditionally forgive you, and give you permission to no longer carry this burden.

It is important to write this in pen. It needs to be hand written, you also need to sign it. Write this letter to yourself, sign it, then read it to yourself. Then set it on fire, and let it be gone forever.

You owe yourself that.

I can't stress the importance of this exercise enough. I know it may seem like it's an easy exercise that isn't very effective, but it is powerful.

Sergeant Smith was a Soldier that I had never met before his squad brought him to me. When they brought him out of the HMMWV, his head was wrapped in a bandage and he was unresponsive.

When the bandage was taken off to expose his wounds, pieces of his brain fell out with it. He had taken a 7.62 round to his head. He was dead, and there wasn't anything anybody could have done to save him. The best doctor in the world wouldn't have been able to help.

Yet, I blamed myself. For well over 3 years I hated myself for not being able to save him.

This will seem unreal to those who have not experienced it, but he would haunt me in my dreams. I would see him lying on the stretcher, reaching up and saying "Save me". This was one of the worst nightmares that I would experience. It would happen about twice a week.

Since I have done that exercise, I haven't had that nightmare, not even once.

That's how powerful this was to me, and I hope that it can do the same for you.

I would also like to add that the flipside of this coin is what is known as survivor's guilt. I personally struggled with this when I came back. I lost friends over there who were casualties that I was unable to save.

So why me? Why did I make it back? I was just a twenty-something year old guy that was single. Why did I make it back when there were Soldiers that had family that didn't make it back. It didn't make any sense.

That last line pretty much sums it all up… It didn't make any sense.

There is no algorithm over there that states that you are better off to die because you don't have family back home. There isn't a checklist that the enemy goes by, where the sniper is getting ready to take the shot and his superior officer comes over and says "Hey, don't shoot that one, he has a one year old at home."

It's WAR. They are just trying to kill the bad guy, just like you. Don't feel bad that you made it back and your buddy didn't. It was a crap shoot on who died and who didn't.

Over time, you will be able to realize that you don't have anything to be guilty about. Over time, you will realize that it wasn't your fault.

I also hope that you realize that the best thing you can do to honor your buddy that didn't make it back is to live your life to the fullest. He or she is probably looking down at you right now smiling. Hell, they are probably saying to themselves "It's about time that knucklehead got help so that he or she can start living their lives." They are probably smiling because they know you are on your path to honor them by living your life to the fullest.

6,000 MILE
SNIPER SHOT

"People don't commit suicide because they don't want to live, they commit suicide because they don't know how to stop the pain".

To this day, I still don't know if this is a quote that I read somewhere or if it was a realization that popped into my head. Regardless, it's powerful.

Statistically, 22 Veterans will commit suicide every day.

That means every day a Veteran does an assessment of their lives and decides they are better off eating a bullet or slitting their wrists or jumping off a bridge than they are living in the country they fought to protect.

Where did we go wrong? Where is the breakdown?

I strongly believe it is in the transition process. I think ALL of this can be avoided.

While there are numerous reasons people commit suicide, with the exception of money problems, the largest one is psychological.

Where are we failing our troops so miserably that they are committing suicide in record numbers?

I think the problem is twofold.

1. These Veterans are leaving active duty thinking their PTSD is just a sign of them being weak. They aren't being shown clear, medical evidence that it is a physical INJURY. It's a completely different perspective to look at it as being weak as opposed to looking at it as being something that you need treatment for. If every day we were finding 22 people dead on the ground from blood loss, we would do some investigating. If those results were to show that they were stabbed earlier in the day, we would wonder why they didn't get medical treatment. However, we will never have that scenario unfold because being stabbed is a physical injury that is widely known. (If you get stabbed, you need to go to the hospital to get fixed). It is absolutely mind blowing that we are still finding 22 bodies on the ground every day and not

doing something about it. The DOD needs to better educate our returning Veterans. But we still can't just point fingers, we need to hold them accountable, demand change and also do whatever we can on our ends to break down the stigma attached to PTSD.

2. We need to hold our VA accountable. To the troops who do go there to get help, they have already won an extremely large internal battle within themselves. They have swallowed their pride and are ready to get treatment. However, the VA is a bureaucracy that has no oversight. We hear over and over again about the VA losing records or putting Veterans on kill lists or performing medical malpractice, etc. But there are almost NEVER any consequences for their actions! It's almost like we get to the point where we are used to seeing it on TV and we brush it off. This is unacceptable! The only time when they should have been giving ANY room for padding should have been when the Global War on Terror began and we thought it would be a short conflict. In a way, it was understandable that the VA was overwhelmed with patients at first, but that excuse can only last for so long. There should have been a time when they adjusted fire and hired new employees. I say that as

an Iraq War Veteran, but I say it with boiling blood in my body for all of the previous war Veterans who do not have a voice.

Since we can come to the conclusion that PTSD is a large contributor to the Veteran suicide rate, we need to come to a solution. I have listed two above, but nearly this entire book is a series of small things that I utilized to get back from a very dark place.

In 2009, I almost took my own life. I was done. I felt hopeless. I didn't understand PTSD and I thought I was being weak, I thought I was being a little bitch. I was tired of everything reminding me of Iraq, I was tired of nightmares nearly every night. I just wanted it all to end. I sat on my couch and put a loaded pistol in my mouth. It then dawned on me that I had pushed everybody away. I didn't have any friends and it would be my sister and my niece that would find my dead body so I decided to overdose on pills instead. I miscalculated the dosage and ended up just falling asleep. I awoke the next morning and a series of events lead me to the Vet Center that I mentioned in this book that literally saved my life. But I just wanted to share that with you because if you are reading this book and have even the tiniest sliver of a thought going through your head about committing suicide, you need to understand that I've been there.

I've fought those demons and I hope this book helps pull you back from that dark place. I truly hope it does. I type this with tears in my eyes because I know that it seems that there is no hope. You don't want to die but you don't know how to end the pain. It gets better. Every single day your life can get just 1% better and before you know it, the dark days will seem like a distant memory. Stand with me and let's choose the sun.

Let's show the enemies that they WON'T win this fight. That they aren't going to be able to celebrate our loss. That they aren't getting a 6,000 mile sniper shot on us. That we kicked their ass on their own soil and they won't bring the fight into our homes and into our minds.

It all starts with making the choice. It all starts with making the choice to fight this fight. One person can make a difference and by you choosing to live, you may inspire another to do the same and that person, etc. Choose to fight beside me, choose to be my brother, choose to stand with me in the sun.

THE GREATEST DRUG OF THEM ALL

Adrenaline is a drug.

What I see a LOT with returning Veterans is that they self-medicate when they get home. Sometimes it's marijuana, sometimes it's alcohol, sometimes it's coke, sometimes it's sex, sometimes it's over-eating, etc.

I certainly drank my fair share of beer when I returned and I cover that in a different chapter. But my real drug, the one that I was addicted to and needed as much as I could get, was adrenaline.

We have all experienced adrenaline before, maybe when we had to read out loud in middle school, our first fight, or when we had to show our parents our grade card that had an F on it, etc.

It wasn't until Iraq that I got the GOOD stuff. The uncut, high quality adrenaline that you aren't going to find in day to day experiences that I recognized my addiction.

I can tell you one thing – I have NEVER had a bigger high than when I was standing over a casualty and we were both covered in blood, a combination of blood and sweat was dripping down my face, the casualty was screaming out, pleading to God, the Blackhawk helicopter coming in hot out of fear of being shot down with an RPG and I was worried about taking a sniper round to my head.

Words can't describe it, in no way was it enjoyable, but to get that feeling again - I'd do anything.

So I searched for it when I got home. Fighting, skydiving, jiu-jitsu tournaments, racing cars, zip-lining, you name it and if I thought I could get a high off of it, I'd do it immediately. I was truly a junkie.

I still do some of that stuff, but I now do it because I enjoy jumping out of an airplane every once in a while. It's not me going there to get my fix. It doesn't control me.

How did things change? Well, when you can increase the quality of the other areas of your life, you won't have to fill it in with this high. You won't be miserable looking for that release, for that small amount of time when you can be high and happy. You will feel happy all throughout the day. It will be a different kind of high, a healthier high.

IT'S OKAY TO CRY

It's ok to cry. Yes, I'm talking to you. It's a natural thing that human beings do. It's not just for girls or for weak people, or "emo" kids.

EVERYBODY CRIES.

Circa 2009, if someone were to ask me if I cry, I would flat out deny it. Yet that was the darkest of my days. It was when I was battling the strongest demons in my fight against PTSD. At least once a week I would just break down and completely lose it. I would bawl like a little baby.

Yet, I would never admit it. Never in a million years.

Why? Because I was a tough Soldier. I was a man's man, I wasn't weak.

But the truth is, I was weak back then. Not for crying, but for not having the courage to admit that I cried. What takes more strength? To say "I'm not a pussy, I don't cry!" or to find the courage to admit to it?

I've got another one of those crazy experiments for you. EMBRACE IT.

It's a great release because we all build up stress and sadness. If you just keep building it up without releasing it, one day you'll explode.

About once a month, or when I feel it may be necessary, I go all out. I put on some sad music, and I bring up all the sad moments that have recently happened in my life and many major sad moments from the past and I just experience it. I don't let myself get pissed off, I don't let myself get sad, I don't let myself get happy. I just allow those experiences to present themselves and whatever emotion pops up, pops up.

It's a great release and sometimes I cry and sometimes I don't. But the thing is, showing my vulnerable side is something I'm not great at, so during this dedicated time block of my life, I am able to release.

Give this exercise a shot. You'll feel better at the end. Crying doesn't make you weak, it makes you HUMAN.

IT HAPPENS

If you ask a majority of men what they would consider to be an embarrassing moment for themselves, the following two would likely rank highly:

Crying

Crapping their pants

I have helped over 1,000 Veterans transition back to civilian life. I've been on both ends of the spectrum. Sometimes they would just swing into the office and would need a form to fill out to send into the VA. The other end of that would be having deep conversations with them, I have probably heard some things from Veterans that they haven't even told their closest family members.

I think that's because they knew I was another Veteran that had deployed. A Veteran that could relate to them, and I usually could. In some way, I could understand what they were going through. I may not be able to understand the fear and anxiety right before you breach a door and could possibly end up face to face with a man who was going to try and kill you, but I understood the fear and anxiety when the radio was keyed and over it came "ATTENTION ALL BUCKEYE MEDICS, WE HAVE 3 INCOMING CASUALTIES. ALL MEDICS REPORT TO THE AID STATION". Because you never knew if they would be incoming casualties with superficial wounds due to an ineffective IED that just hit them with some shrapnel, or if you were going to be dealing with amputations and have a 19 year old kid begging you to save his life so he could make it back to his wife and kid.

That last sentence got away from me, but I just want to stress the point that I was never dumbfounded. That there was never an instance where I couldn't relate to a Veteran at least on some level.

Until one time I was hanging out with an Infantry Marine. I now forget what exactly the setting was, but we were having a couple beers. He looked over at me and said "Hey Doc, you ever shit your pants when you were scared over there?"

I was speechless. I had never heard of any cases of this happening before. I've talked to TONS of Veterans, and I've heard of them vomiting after killing someone but never about soiling themselves. Furthermore, the handful of books out there on PTSD didn't mention anything about it at all. So really, at that point, I just said "No, I haven't, but people deal with stress in different ways."

That's because I was ignorant. That's because I think that this fact is a bigger stigma than admitting you have PTSD. Soiling yourself when you are exposed to extreme combat is just as common as auditory exclusion (when all of the sounds are muffled). It's a natural body response. 25% of World War II Soldiers admitted to defecating themselves in combat.

If this is so common, then why was this the first I heard about it? Well, it wasn't until I read Lt. Col. Dave Grossman's book "On Combat" that I had heard these facts. His book is definitely a must read if you want to learn more about the physiological changes that happen to your body during combat. I don't say that lightly. He's an Army Ranger and Psychologist that speaks on only what he knows and can back up his research with historical facts and statistics.

In short, I included this chapter because this book has power. It will make its way into numerous Veterans hands. Some will just want to help ease their transition to civilian life, some will want help dealing with the things they saw in combat, but hopefully there is ONE that is wondering if it is normal that he shit his pants during a firefight or an explosion. The answer is YES. Don't be ashamed of a natural reaction that takes place in your body.

GONE BUT NOT FORGOTTEN

Everybody will die. That's just the way it is, but not everybody will be forgotten.

Losing someone you know in combat is indescribable, and something you can't explain to somebody that hasn't experienced it.

I think it's because while we've all been to many funerals in our lives, there is something different knowing there was a person who took your friend from you. That there was someone who pulled the trigger or detonated the bomb that killed your brother or sister. That their lives were taken needlessly.

That's a difficult thing to live with, I know. But I hope you understand that the biggest way you can honor them is to not let them be forgotten. They touched you in a special way and made incredible contributions to this world.

They were the good in what can sometimes be an ugly place.

You may be asking me how I know this if I have never met you, let alone them. Well they wouldn't be on your mind if they weren't special.

History books will only remember Hitler for the evil things that he did. Nobody will ever say "Hey, that Adolf guy would give you the shirt off his back." Nor would they say "I really miss Osama Bin Laden, he was a great guy."

But, your fallen brother or sister is on your mind for a reason. While they may be dead, do not let them be forgotten. Share their story and speak of them when you get the chance. Tell people how great they were. Tell how they touched or inspired you. Tell how they used to make you laugh.

Tell your family about how they would always be upbeat and happy. Even during recall formations and redundant weapon cleanings.

Tell the people at your church how they were so selfless and would always be willing to help anybody and everybody.

Tell the guys at the VFW about that time you passed out early and they drew a dick on your face with a sharpie.

Your friend will never die as long as your keep him or her alive in your heart.

YOU ARE GREAT, DON'T FORGET THAT

Right now if I were to ask you to list all of your failures, you could probably talk my ear off. You could go on and on and on about all of the things that you failed at in your life.

Why? Because the military has trained us to focus more on our failures than our successes. It's few and far between to be recognized when you do positive things in the military. But when you do wrong, you'll never live it down.

How many times did your Drill Sergeant tell you "Good Job, Bucko!" It's likely that didn't happen.

But I bet you can recall that time you were shark attacked for one of your blouse buttons being undone, or your bootlace hanging out.

I bet you can recall that time you were smoked because you couldn't remember your General Orders.

I bet you can remember that time Drill Sergeant destroyed your wall locker for leaving it unlocked.

But it doesn't stop at basic. Have you ever been smoked for being late for formation? Ever had to do extra duty for making a mistake?

I don't think any of these are wrong. I mean there are some pretty silly things that go on in the military (recall formations for the private that got a DUI, that ironically won't even be at the recall formation).

I think these are necessary to keep the discipline that is needed in a Soldier. Unfortunately, the psychological effects remain when you leave, and they are harming to your psyche.

That's why you can recall your failures more vividly then you can your successes.

That's why you have forgotten how great you are!

So I ask you to do this challenge. Split your life in half, not your military career, but your life.

If you are 40 years old then you would have your first half (1-20) and your second half (21-40). Now list 5 achievements that you have had in each half.

Do this on a physical piece of paper, not a computer or a smart phone. Then keep that piece of paper and add one achievement per week at a minimum, you can even do it daily! Most successful people have one of these, they call it a success log.

Sometimes they will be large achievements and sometimes they may be small things, but remember that even the small things are achievements and are worth recognizing!

The idea is to shift your thought process from focusing on your failures to focusing on your achievements. This is powerful and will change your life. You will notice a change in your self-esteem.

Also, create a special place in your house or office where you will put all of your objects that will remind you of your successes. A place that you will walk by every day and see your medals and anything else you were rewarded with in the military. Add in all of trophies and things that you received prior to your military days and have achieved since then. Break out your old ribbons from when you did that 5k. Your employee of the month award, your college degree, your picture of you standing on a beach in Florida, your badge from Boy Scouts or Girl Scouts, etc.

Your environment has a HUMONGOUS effect on you.

Walking by that designated place every day will help reprogram your mind. To help you remember how great you are and of everything you have accomplished.

It's not being arrogant, it's not being full of yourself. These are all things that YOU have earned. Break them out, shine them up and put them on display. You deserve to constantly be reminded of how great you are!

FIND YOUR TRUE NORTH

You have to find your true north. You have to find what makes you happy. It's like when you're issued a compass, just because it points north doesn't mean it's correct. You know that magnetic declination will throw off your true north a bit, and you will have to adjust depending on where you are in the world. The same is true with what will truly make you happy. I can't answer that for you, the VA can't answer that for you, your friends can't answer that for you. Only YOU know what that is and actually, you may not even truly know yet. But hopefully I can help you find out.

I go to a tremendous amount of self-development workshops. It started off as a way to better myself but quickly turned into not only a way to help myself, but to pass that information on and help others.

Regardless, something common that you will find in the better workshops is an exercise that will help you see what you truly want.

It works like this:

You have someone ask you "What do you want?" for five minutes straight.

It sounds simple, but it really isn't. In the beginning it is easy and you'll say things like:

I want a million dollars.

I want a new car.

I want a big house.

I want a pool.

But then you'll start to slow down a bit and you'll have to dig deeper. This is when you will start to learn more about yourself. I pretty much had the above answers when I first started out, but about halfway through I was drawing blanks and my partner kept asking me what I wanted and I started blurting out things that I never in a million years would have said out loud. It just came out.

I want to be able to love again.

I want someone to tell me they're proud of me.

I want the pain to go away.

I want to make a difference in this world.

I want a family.

Do this with someone that you are comfortable with because to be 100% honest, I was crying like a little bitch by the end of it. I hesitated on putting that in here because I was worried it may scare you from doing the exercise, but then I decided to put it in because it really works.

Man, I'm putting myself out there. I really did cry like a little bitch, and you might too. But you will feel better, and you'll have a better idea of what you want in life. What you TRULY want in life.

The first time I did this, I wanted to dig deeper and learn more about myself when I got home, but I was single, still a knucklehead, and too stubborn to ask someone to help me. So I recorded myself saying "WHAT DO YOU WANT?!?!" for 5 minutes straight, then played it back to myself.

I want you to find your true north. I see so many people going through life using someone else's compass. They're trying to make a million bucks, or are going to college to be a doctor and have no desire to be in the medical field. As you know, the farther you go without correcting for magnetic declination, the farther you will be from where you want to be.

I want you to be happy. I want you to find home. Do the exercise. Adjust your azimuth, and steer your way to a life that will make you happy.

SET GOALS

You can't get to where you want to be if you don't know two things:

1. Where you are.
2. Where you want to go.

I often hear a lot of people, not just Veterans, talk about how they are unhappy with their results in life. But if you ask them what they want then they will respond with something like "Well, I don't know. I've never really thought about it. I'm just not happy with where I'm at now".

Think about that - you're unhappy with your life and you haven't decided where you want to go, but you're unhappy that you aren't there!

Your life is similar to using a GPS system. In order to get from where you are to where you want to be, you need to do the following things:

Find out where you currently are.

Decide where you would like to go.

Press on the gas!

Of course that's the simplified version of it, it may not be THAT easy. Along the way you might encounter a blocked road or get a flat tire, but those are all insignificant setbacks. As long as you stay focused, you will arrive at your destination!

Remember, commercial airplanes are off track more than 90% of the time but still arrive at their destinations because they know EXACTLY where they are heading. If the winds shift or they are off track, they just make small corrections along the way.

Do some soul-searching and find out what you truly want in life. Do you want to make more money? Do you want to lose weight? Have a better relationship with your partner? Compete in a race?

Well if you said yes to any of those, I have good news and bad news for you.

The good news is that you can accomplish any of those.

The bad news is that you can accomplish any of those.

Now I bet you're really confused, aren't you?

Well goal-setting needs to be SPECIFIC. Do you want to make more money? How about if your boss gave you a ten cent an hour raise? That would be more money, wouldn't it?

Goals need to have a clear finish line, so to speak. You can lie to yourself if you set a very generic goal. You can either accept that ten cent an hour raise and be happy with it because you met your "goal", or your only other option would be to NOT be happy with it and have to talk to your boss and demand that promotion you truly want.

Let's take a look at some more effective ways to set goals.

"I want to run a race" could be "On February 27th, I will cross the finish line at the ABC 5k race".

"I want to lose weight" would be more effective if you wrote down "On January 10th, at 5:00pm I will weigh 180 pounds".

"I want to have a better relationship with my family" would be more effective if you wrote down "Every Thursday, I will turn off my phone and we will do an activity and have dinner as a family".

See the difference in the way the goals are written? One goal could be perceived a million different ways by a million different people. The other way is more definitive. On your goals date, either you will weigh 180 or you won't. Either you ran the race you wrote down, or you didn't.

Now, I am trying to shy away from statistics in this book because I think they are only as good as their sources. I also think many statistics are flawed. However, there is one statistic that stays pretty common across the board, and that's if you write down your goals you are FAR more likely to achieve them as opposed to someone that hasn't.

If you share them with the world, you are FAR more likely to achieve them than the person who just writes them down.

So what is your goal? What is it that you want to accomplish?

You are more powerful than you think. You can literally create the life you want to have. Do you want to have a great job? Do you want to live in a nice house? Do you want to run a marathon? Do you want to write a book?

You can accomplish anything you want, but it all starts with making it a goal.

SWEET DREAMS

For many of you out there with PTSD, it's not only difficult to fall asleep, but it's scary to even think about.

You do whatever it takes to fight the Z-monster. You do whatever it takes to not lose and let your eyelids shut because while your daily life may not be great, it's paradise compared to the nightmares you experience when you fall asleep.

Ghosts were waiting for me, casualties were blaming me for not saving them. Vivid, realistic experiences of treating casualties would replay in mind.

Hell, there was even a couple of times where I would have a nightmare inside a nightmare. This was before the Inception movie came out. You want to talk about something you don't want to tell ANYBODY about? You want to seriously doubt if you are sane? Hell, at the time I didn't even tell my counselor about that.

Well, I've got some good news. You can stop a large majority of the nightmares you are experiencing. I know you are thinking, if it was that easy you would already do it. The truth is, you can. You have to couple what I'm about to tell you with the chapter on "break the cycle".

When we sleep, we don't use our conscious mind. If we did, we would dream about being rich and petting puppies and all kinds of wonderful things. We would be able to guide our dreams more effectively.

When we are asleep, we use our subconscious mind. We use the part of our brain that we continue to program when we are awake. When we're awake, we are continuously putting information into our subconscious mind. I won't get too much into the neuroscience behind it, but if we spend all day putting bad things into it, when we fall asleep, that's all our subconscious mind has to pull from. That's why so much in this book is important for you to not only understand, but to put into practice. To live a healthy life with PTSD, we essentially have to reprogram our underlying belief system.

There are also a couple of things we can do right before we go to sleep that can help. Think of when you were a little kid (before you had any bad experiences). You would go to sleep and dream about magical things or not dream at all. That's because your subconscious mind hadn't been programmed yet.

However, there were a few incidents when you would have nightmares. They weren't consistent, they were every once in a while. So why did they occur? If you look back, you can remember exactly why they occurred. Chances are, in the hour or so before bedtime, you created an imaginary situation in your head (conscious) that carried over to your dreams (subconscious).

You knew for a FACT that there was a monster in the closet, so when you fell asleep, you had a nightmare about a monster.

You watched a scary movie before you went to bed, then replayed the scary parts of that movie in your head until you fell asleep, you then had nightmares about a serial killer or a ghost.

I'm not trying to insult your intelligence here, you can obviously understand that if you think about something scary before you go to bed, you will dream about it.

Well, even though we know that, I know a lot of Veterans that are essentially creating their own nightmares. I know I did it for the longest time.

We can reprogram ourselves at the fundamental level by doing some of the techniques in this book, but right before we go to sleep, we can shift our mindset.

I know that I used to revisit the thoughts and experiences of the day right before I went to sleep. Sometimes I would also replay some bad memories of Iraq while I was in bed. I would CONTINUALLY have terrifying nightmares. At the time, I couldn't understand it. However, in hindsight, it makes perfect sense now. I was creating my dreams by creating images in my mind right before I fell asleep. (Think little kid watching a scary movie).

You can very easily shift your thoughts and cut down on so many nightmares. I know this because I've done it and have helped a lot of others do it.

Start thinking of something peaceful before you go to sleep. Think about being in a hammock on the beach. Not a care in the world. Nobody else around. Just you laying in the hammock. Inhale and exhale deeply. Let nothing come into your mind. Just let happiness enter your body as you hear the waves lapping in. Repeat until you fall asleep.

You will see a HUGE change in the content of your dreams.

Now some psychology books will tell you to visualize tomorrow going just as you want it. I mean, that's an option and you can try it, but it didn't work for me. I'd start visualizing waking up and the day starting off good and then somebody at the supermarket would say something stupid and I'd get frustrated and angry and I wouldn't fall asleep. I would just get pissed off and lay in bed awake and angry.

I have to tell you though, in the beginning the beach thing didn't work for me. There was just too much going on in my head for me to focus. If I tried to visualize anything, it would eventually lead back to something I didn't want to think about.

I found a method that worked for me. I would visualize animals starting at A and going to Z. This method didn't allow me to stray in either direction. It was a good medium ground when I was trying to figure all of this out. I would just start with A and name an animal and go all the way to Z. I would then repeat that. This kind of neutralized my brain while also keeping it mildly active, but not to the point where it would keep me awake. Yet, the thoughts that were in my head weren't negative. They were just animals. Eventually, I wouldn't have any dreams at all.

I would just close my eyes and visualize an Armadillo, Bird, Cat, Donkey, Elephant, etc.

I then got to the point where I did some of the exercises (that I put in the other chapters) throughout the day, and it changed my subconscious mind to the point where I flooded out the negative thoughts and I could start doing the beach exercise without intrusive thoughts popping up.

I now go to bed and count off a list of things I am grateful for. To the best of my knowledge, I don't have dreams anymore. I just wake up feeling happy and at peace with the world.

YOUR BEDROOM IS FOR SLEEP

Your bedroom is for sleep... and sex.

That's it. You should get rid of all distractions in your bedroom. You are confusing your brain and making it that much harder to get a good night's rest.

The irritability and nightmares can be minimized or even removed with the practices in the previous chapter, but even if you have the capability to get a good night's sleep, you need to create the environment to do so.

Your bedroom is not a work station. It's not a couch in a living room. It's not a dining table. It's a place to do two things and two things only.

We actually confuse our brains when we do something other than use our bedroom to sleep. Our brains think that it's time to actually become engaged and to turn on. Our brains associate lying in bed with time to check Facebook, send a text message, or to watch a television show. It becomes confused, so when you try to lay down and go to sleep, it's in a limbo. Eventually you will fall asleep, but it's a psychological struggle.

So go into your room and make sure that it's in a condition to maximize your ability to sleep.

Take the TV out and put it somewhere else. Don't bring your laptop or tablet to bed with you so you can catch up on "just one more email" before you go to bed. Don't even bring your phone to bed with you. Put the charger in your living room or kitchen. You will just be tempted to check for Facebook updates or to answer an incoming text message.

You may be saying "But I use my phone as an alarm clock".

GO GET A $5 ALARM CLOCK FROM THE STORE!

You should also make your bedroom as dark as possible. This is extremely important as it affects your melatonin levels. So shut your door and turn off all lights (including night lights, etc.).

If you work a night job and can only sleep during the day, try your best to cover the windows with a curtain or purchase black out curtains. The importance of having your room be pitch black with no interruptions cannot be over stressed. An eye mask is also an option to keep light out.

Turn your bedroom into a calming, comfortable haven, where you mind and body know that when your head hits that pillow, it's time to rest and that's it, nothing else.

CONNECT WITH OTHERS

Humans need interaction, that's just the way it is. It's been that way since we were cavemen. It provided us with necessary security. It's in our genes. It's a part of us and to this day, we still need it.

However, most Veterans self-isolate. If there is something I'm an expert on, it's this.

I self-isolated when I first got back because other people aggravated me. They just didn't understand me, and they always wanted to talk politics. So I self-isolated from people I knew. Then the public aggravated me. Listening to a lady yell at the cashier because she wouldn't take her twenty cent coupon made my blood boil. I guess I slowly lost interest in wanting to be around anybody at all.

So slowly it became normal. It became something I was used to. Just as to a cigarette smoker, smoking 20 cigarettes a day is normal, but to an outsider it's unhealthy. Science proves that it isn't healthy for us and we know it isn't, but we still do it. Smokers don't think twice about it because it's just the norm for them. (I'm not bashing smokers, I smoked for nearly 20 years).

That's how I eventually ended up. I would even go grocery shopping in the middle of the night so I didn't have to interact with anybody, but I was lonely and unhappy.

I hope there is someone out there reading this book that can relate. I know how you're feeling. You aren't a freak of nature, you aren't an outcast, you aren't a bad person. Your body just went into survival mode. You shunned people so you wouldn't get into an argument when politics came up. You quit going to bars with your friends, because you always got into fights. You quit going to places that had a lot of people, because it triggered you. You were scared to go out in public, because you were worried something might trigger you and you'd embarrass yourself....again.

You say that you're happy but you aren't. You're in your comfort zone. You're in a bubble that you have created. A place where nobody can harm you. Deep inside you know you aren't happy, you know that you're lonely. You know that you want to change your life, you just don't know how to.

You feel like you've dug a hole of loneliness and don't know how to get out of it.

Well, it's baby steps. A little at a time. Call up some of your buddies and invite them over for the game. Or call up one of your friends and see if they want to go watch a movie. Start putting yourself back out there.

When I was running my organization, that was a main part of what we did. We had events every month where we would get together and do anything from bowling to festivals. It was easy because everybody was a Veteran, so it was a little less intimidating.

Check out the local AMVETS and VFW's near you. You could also go to meetup.com and join a group that interests you. They have everything from running groups to cooking groups to video game enthusiast groups, etc. If you don't see something that interests you, you could always start your own.

Your life won't change unless you take action. Do at least ONE thing this week that puts you out there with other people, no matter how small it is. Then next week do another, etc. Soon you will be surrounded by great people, and you will wonder how you lived without social interaction.

YOUR FIRE TEAM

I'd like to start this chapter off with a fairly famous quote

"You are the average of the five people you spend the most time with." – Jim Rohn

Remember that quote and do an assessment of who you are surrounding yourself with. Are they bringing you down or helping you become a better person?

They are your new fire team. They are your new squad. They are your new platoon.

Surround yourself with the best people that you possibly can. When you were in the military, you were surrounded by the best. You were held to a standard and so was everybody around you. There might have been some people that bitched, but if you had good leadership, you guys weren't sitting around feeling sorry for yourselves.

This happens a LOT in the civilian world, not only with returning Veterans, but with a majority of the population.

It's something we normally don't think about, we just think that we have a group of friends and that's it. They're OUR friends, we chose them so there's no changing that. It's easy to get stuck in this way of thinking, but you need to break this habit. You need to step back and do an honest assessment. Are the people in your life bringing you down, or helping you be your best?

Are they the ones at work that bitch about their jobs all day, or are they normally upbeat and when you see them, you feel good?

Are your friends supportive of you, or are they always telling you what you CAN'T do? Are they always complaining?

How about your partner if you have one? Do they make you feel incredible when you guys are together? Or are they constantly nagging you? Are they talking down to you and calling you names?

Get out a piece of paper and write down all of the names of the people you interact with throughout a month's time.

Now read the name out loud, visualize them, and write down either a "+" or a "−" sign next to their name.

These are knee jerk reactions, if they make you feel happy, put a "+" next to their name and if they don't make you feel happy or if they bring you down, put a "−" next to their name.

It's important that these are knee jerk reactions. You could very easily have a negative knee jerk reaction when you think about your girlfriend, but then your conscious brain starts making excuses. That's what we do, we try to validate the life choices we've made.

"Sally doesn't make me happy as a partner, but it's better than being lonely."

"Jim talks behind my back, but he's the only person I know that also likes to work on cars."

"The guys at work are always talking about depressing stuff, but the only other option would be to eat alone."

You then need to start spending as little time as possible with the ones that have a "−" next to their name.

THEY ARE POISON. There's no other way to put it. They are slowly killing you.

I know because that's what I did when I first got back. I hung out with my friends from high school. At this point, we were all in our late 20's and most of them were still living with their parents and getting drunk and smoking weed every weekend. We became friends in high school because we all came from broken homes. Our mentality at the time was that we were the "outsiders" and that we were destined to not achieve anything because that was only reserved for the "rich kids who had mommy and daddy hand them everything."

They were toxic to me. They didn't have any ambitions in life and I slowly adopted that mentality as well. Once I quit hanging out with them I started to feel like I wanted to do great things. Like I could make a difference in this world. I didn't know how at the time, but I had that inspiration when I decided not to hang out with them anymore. I honestly believe I never would have written this book if I still had them in my social circle.

I then had to once again, make a tough decision and end a relationship I was in. That one definitely wasn't easy. I didn't want to be lonely, but she wasn't supportive of me at the time. This was a while ago when I didn't know any coping mechanisms to deal with my PTSD, and she wasn't supportive when I wanted to try new things to live a happier life. Example: Going to a local bar with live music but if I needed to leave, I NEEDED to leave right then. The band started singing death metal and moshing. I told her I needed to leave and she said "No, I want to stay and watch this next show". I finally made the decision to break that one off when I was outside in the fetal position and she was still inside watching the band finish. That was hard because I didn't want to be lonely, but it was necessary for me to ULTIMATELY be happy.

Sometimes that's what is needed to find ultimate happiness. Sometimes you need to let go of the toxic people in your life to allow room for the good people to enter. This isn't easy, but it is ABSOLUTELY necessary.

MAKE COPIES OF YOUR COPIES

Make copies of everything that you have. I mean make a LOT of copies. Make at least five copies of your military records and keep them in various places. Keep a copy in your safe, a copy at your parent's house, a copy in your safe deposit box, etc.

This is something that was told to me by a Vietnam Veteran who learned everything the hard way.

He submitted his original copies of everything to the VA and they lost them. All of his records were gone. Discharge papers, sick call slips, awards, everything was gone in a blink of an eye because the VA employees misplaced them.

There are numerous reports of the VA doing this, but you should also keep copies just because you never know when you might need them. Will you need them for state benefits? Will you need them for a Veteran discount? You might just want to have the copies so you can show them to your children or grandchildren someday.

You may have them now, but will you still have them 15 years down the road when you have moved several times?

What if you only have one copy and they get destroyed in a fire?

What if your boyfriend or girlfriend gets pissed off at you and throws everything out in the rain?

This is an extremely cheap thing that you can do, and the $5 or however much it takes to make the copies is a well spent investment since you will have peace of mind.

GO TO A VET CENTER

I wouldn't be here today if it wasn't for my local Vet Center. You can make your own assumptions about the VA and I have heard both horror stories and I have heard good stories. It seems that VA's are similar to individual units where if they have squared away command structures then they are effective.

I've never heard of a Vet Center being jacked up, not one story. This may seem confusing at first because Vet Centers are actually a part of the VA. Well, they are funded by the VA, but once you walk in you will be able to tell that it's a totally different world.

Most Vet Centers are staffed by other Combat Veterans, so some of the frustrations of the VA aren't there. You won't have a civilian who treats you like you're a burden or some psychiatrist that is right out of med school that insults your intelligence.

I went to the Vet Center as a last resort after I had a very unhappy experience with the VA. They actually assigned me a psychiatrist who was Middle Eastern. At the time, that was one of the worst things they could have possibly done. I mean, I understand that accidents happen sometimes, but holy crap, assign an Iraq War Veteran a psychiatrist that speaks broken English?!?

So, I decided to give the Vet Center a shot and was very happy with what they had to offer. My counselor was a Combat Marine that served in Iraq just a few years before I did. He was able to relate to me and understand a lot of what I was saying. He really helped me by not only listening to what I was saying, but by sharing his own experiences of what helped him readjust to civilian life.

The Vet Center also has tons of other services that they offer. They can help you with applying for VA benefits, filing a claim, readjustment counseling, PTSD services, etc. They do family counseling as well.

I'm sure that I didn't cover EVERYTHING they offer, but a quick Google search will help you find your local Vet Center. Locate it, stop by and tell them you want to learn a little more about what they have to offer. Chances are, you'll be pleasantly surprised.

GET HELP WITH YOUR RESUME

Go fix your resumé. It doesn't do you justice and your potential employers don't understand it.

I can say that with a certain amount of confidence because at the organization I used to run, I would have Veterans that would come in and want help with their resumés. The average one would look something like this:

Joe Soldier
U.S. Army 03SEP2001-03SEP2005
Infantry

> Neutralized threats
> Cleaned and maintained weapon
> Provided security

Now I love infantry jokes just as much as the next guy, but you guys did so much more than just kick down doors and shoot people. You were a trainer and a mentor to other

Soldiers. How many thousands, if not hundreds of thousands of dollars worth of equipment were you responsible for? Didn't you plan and execute training classes for your Joes? Didn't you prepare reports like AARs, Supply Requests, Risk Assessments, OPORDs, etc.? Weren't you responsible for operating under pressure? Didn't you have to work as a team and communicate daily to your chain of command? Didn't you have to "counsel" bad "employees" and train them to properly do their job? These are just a couple of examples, but you have an incredible amount of leadership skills that go far beyond "Shot guns and killed bad guys".

You also have to communicate in a way that employers (who aren't Veterans) can understand. Most won't understand when you say, "It was my responsibility to PMCS the M998" or "It was my responsibility to keep my Class A's in inspectable condition IAW AR-670-1". You might as well be speaking a foreign language to someone who wasn't in the military. Talk in terms they can understand. "It was my responsibility to maintain and keep our military vehicles in working order on a daily basis", or "It was my responsibility to keep my dress uniform in an inspectable condition per Army regulations". These are just a couple of examples, but hopefully you get my point.

This isn't specific to infantry, it was few and far between that I saw a Veteran with a resumé who truly communicated all of the assets they have to offer an employer. Please do yourself a favor and go to a VFW or some place that can help you with your resumé. Going to the Vet Center that I have mentioned in this book would be a great place to start.

As a Veteran, you are an incredible asset to any employer. You have an incredible work ethic and solid skills that most employers WANT. Just tighten up your resumé so they can see the value in hiring you.

Also go get a decent email address. Would you want to hire someone who's email address was **ThunderDong69@ internet.com**? Yes, I had a Veteran come in with an email address similar to that printed on his resumé. God bless the infantry.

THE BENEFITS YOU EARNED

I would strongly encourage you to go to the VA and claim every single injury that you ever received while you were on active duty. I mean, ANY injury that you ever had. This includes injuries that don't even bother you anymore.

I could write an entire book about how to apply for VA benefits, but I won't. Truth be told, even when I ran my organization to help Veterans, I would pass them off to the local VFW or AMVETS to have them help with their VA claim. A majority of those places have VSO's (Veteran Service Officers) that are trained to help with claims. They are rock stars at what they do.

So back to claiming EVERY injury that you ever had, I do mean EVERY injury. If you stubbed your toe one night at the barracks, claim it. If you had your jaw broken in a fist fight with another Private, claim it. If you fell during a run and jacked up your knee, claim it even if it doesn't hurt you right now.

Why would you claim your knee if it isn't currently hurting you? Because now it is service connected. Now you have submitted the paperwork and fought the fight to prove that it was injured and related to your military service. So if it starts acting up on you 10 years from now, you can walk right into the VA and get care for it. I can't stress this enough, go to the VA as soon as possible and claim EVERY injury that you ever received while in service.

Another common myth is that you get paid for all of your injuries, you may be thinking to yourself "My knee doesn't hurt, I don't want to get money for something that isn't a big deal". Well, you can be rated 0% for an injury. You can prove your injury and get it service connected. When it comes time to do the exam in which they determine what percentage disabled you are, tell them it doesn't hurt at all at this time. You will be rated at 0% but you will be service connected.

Or maybe you do have an injury that is painful to you, then you should definitely file a claim and get service connected and some money for it each month. YOU EARNED THIS. When you signed your name on the dotted line, you signed a contract. That you would go to boot camp and go through hell. That you would serve out the length of your contract, and that there is a possibility that you could go to war and die for your country. That is what YOU agreed to. The contract works two ways, the other end of that contract states that if you get injured, you get free care for that. It also states that you will receive compensation every month for your injuries. THIS ISN'T A HANDOUT.

You also aren't pulling from a limited pool of money. I would commonly hear Veterans say "I'm not going to file a claim, I don't want to take money away from someone that really needs it." You aren't taking money from anybody. They aren't digging into another Veterans check to pay you for your service related injuries. They have an infinite amount of money to pay for these claims.

This is something that you have earned. Just as you received a monthly paycheck when you were in, you earned these benefits. Stop by a local VFW or AMVETS and talk to them about filing a claim. The sooner, the better.

APPLY FOR STATE BENEFITS

Your benefits are something that you earned, and while it's common to know that you should apply for VA benefits, most Veterans are shocked to find out that there are a lot of state benefits available to them.

It will differ from state to state, but go to a resource that can point you in the right direction (the Vet Center is a great place).

You may get exemptions on your taxes.

You may get free or discounted license plates.

You may get discounted/free hunting and fishing licenses.

I was surprised that I was eligible to receive TWO bonuses through my state equaling over $2,000. The money had been there the entire time, I just didn't know about it until I went to the Vet Center and they told me.

Your state will likely be different than mine, but do some digging around, you'd be surprised what you might find.

DON'T WORK YOUR LIFE AWAY

The mind truly is an amazing thing.

When I was in Combat Medic School, I would always be in awe at how our bodies had certain mechanisms built in that kept us alive.

Our heart rate and our breathing are done behind the scenes. It's so vital to our survival that we don't have to continuously force our hearts to contract and expand to pump blood for us to stay alive. We don't have to continuously force ourselves to inhale and exhale to get the oxygen that we need.

When we get cut, our bodies will automatically retract blood vessels and vasoconstrict (shrink them) to minimize bleeding. Many of our minor wounds will actually heal themselves with little to no intervention at all. The human body is a miraculous machine and our mind is no different.

At the start of the wars in Iraq and Afghanistan, the VA saw a huge uprise in the amount of Vietnam Veterans that were seeking help for PTSD. It was commonly believed that the "new" wars triggered underlying PTSD that most of these Vietnam Veterans didn't know that they had. That the wars unearthed suppressed memories that these brave warriors were pushing back.

That was the thought process for the longest time. That would make logical sense to most people. Because what else could cause all of these Veterans to seek help after nearly 30 years of not showing any signs of PTSD?

Well recently, some incredible theories have been presented that I believe could be very accurate.

These Vietnam Veterans didn't return to a time where the VA was waiting to treat them for PTSD. They didn't return to a land that thanked them for their service and hosted parades. Hell, many of them didn't even mention their service out of fear of being called a baby killer.

They did the best they could with what they had. They sucked it up and found a job. They worked that job the best they could and put everything they had into it. They worked that job for... nearly 30 years.

See, at the time, when the wars in Iraq and Afghanistan were kicking off, many of these Vietnam Veterans were retiring.

Some recent theories point to the possibility that these Veterans bodies (minds) did what was necessary to survive. As our vessels vasoconstrict and retract to slow the blood to keep us alive, these Veterans became workaholics so they didn't have to think of the horrors of combat. It was their body keeping them alive. It was them subconsciously self-medicating. It was a psychological survival mechanism.

This is mind blowing if you think about it. It is also likely that Veterans of earlier conflicts did the same thing. With that information being available to us, it is safe to say that there's a real possibility that current war Veterans will fall into that same trap. That's why I feel this chapter is important to add to this book. I don't have a perfect answer to this problem. I think this book is a good start in the right direction. I think it will open a dialogue for discussion that is needed. I hope it helps raise awareness and gets us searching for answers so we can break this pattern.

A TIME AND A PLACE

What's the difference between a dead hooker and a Ferrari?

I don't have a Ferrari in my garage.

If you laughed at that, then you're a lot different than the people in the self-development seminar I just attended, because they definitely didn't think that was funny.

That was an awkward weekend. I share that particular moment, because that happened just a couple of weekends ago. That was one of my MILDER jokes, I was holding back and they still got offended. They would have lost their minds if I would have pulled out the good stuff.

I think that's why I decided to do this chapter, because if you served in the military, you heard jokes ten times worse than that. I mean at times it seems like it is a contest to see who can make the most inappropriate, filthy, disgusting jokes.

It seems that outside of the military, those jokes aren't funny. So I guess my advice to you on this is just to tone it down a bit. I mean, I got out in 2008 and I'm still toning it down, but just a couple of weeks ago, I could tell I hit a nerve with some of those people. Here we are 8 years later and I'm still trying to figure it out.

There's nothing wrong with you. It's just that the dark humor in the military just isn't appropriate in the civilian world.

For me, this was a big conundrum that confirmed I wasn't going to ever fit back into society, until I understood that there was just a different dynamic. That the humor that we experienced in the military was just specific to the military and that the civilian world has a different gauge of appropriateness.

As you transition into civilian life, don't let your sense of humor die. You can still find a group of Veterans that are going to be able to match you dirty joke for dirty joke. Your sense of humor is a part of you and really it is the only part of me that remained through my battle with PTSD.

Live. Love. LAUGH.

PRACTICE FORGIVENESS

Forgive those that have done you wrong.

I know your knee jerk reaction may be to think I'm crazy for saying that, but it's not doing you any good. It's just eating away at you.

Have you heard the saying "Holding onto anger is like drinking poison and hoping the other person dies?"

Well the first time I heard that, I thought it was only something hippies said. I thought they were words spoken by a weak man that was trying to justify his cowardness.

But in reality, those words couldn't be more true. Think of someone that you have hated for several years. How many times have you felt angry and disgusted when you think about what they did to you? Probably A LOT. How many times did that hurt THEM? None, not even once.

In a way, they are STILL winning. They are living in your head rent free. Be the better man (or woman) and forgive them. It's not showing weakness. It's not saying they are right. It's not saying you give up.

It's just saying that you care enough about yourself to do what is necessary to be happy.

This doesn't mean you have to forget. This doesn't mean you have to be best friends and go get an ice cream cone together. You don't even have to ever see them again. That includes forgiving them. While it would definitely work to forgive them in person, you can get the same exact results by writing them a letter. From there you can choose to either mail it or not.

Don't underestimate the power of putting a pen to paper. It activates a part of your brain that is different from just saying it out loud.

So you can easily write a letter similar to the following:

SFC XXXX,

I have held anger inside me for the longest time, but today I will let it go. In Iraq, you knew that there were units going outside of the wire without medics. You knew they were going out with unqualified Combat Life Savers. There was a day that my friend's convoy got hit and three of my friends died. That is a convoy that I should have been on. We had sufficient medics and I should have been on that convoy. For years, I hated myself because I blamed myself for not being there to save them. I also hated you for your unwise decisions, as I know it was you that influenced our command. Today, I forgive you. Today, I decide not to hold onto the hate anymore. Today, I choose to be free.

Then you sign it and date it. You can mail it to the recipient if you want, but you don't have to. If you choose not to mail it or hand it to the recipient, you should either burn it or crumple it up in your hand and throw it in the trash to signify that it isn't in your life anymore.

I applaud you for your courage, I know it isn't easy, but this will free you from the anger you have been carrying.

TO CARRY OR NOT TO CARRY

"You're one of those crazy war Veterans. There is NO reason for you to carry a gun. You're not in combat anymore".

This isn't a chapter on gun control. This isn't my opinion on the gun laws in this country.

However, it is necessary to address a valid point. An internal dialogue that most Veterans who carry a weapon have and are sometimes perpetuated by their friends and family.

Are you crazy for carrying a weapon?

No, no and no. I was once talking to a buddy of mine and he said to me "The scariest thing about killing someone is how easy it is. Up until that point it was something that just seemed so distant and even though I trained for years for that moment, it just surprised me how it wasn't a big event. How it was so simple".

I share that story because it shows how perspective can really open your eyes and show you a different world. Before I went to Iraq, I had never really seen any serious injuries. As far as violence goes, I had seen many fist fights but they were just that, arguments that were settled with fists.

Iraq opened me up to a world where true violence exists. A world where you can't call time out. A world where you can't call the police. A world where you can't run to your safe space because someone said some mean words to you.

Iraq showed me that there is a world that exists where evil men will kill you for little to no reason at all. A world where one minute, everything can be fine and in a matter of seconds you are fighting for your life, or the life of your buddy. A world where true evil exists.

When I first got home, I applied and got my concealed carry license. Having a weapon on me at all times was reassuring. It was like there was a piece of me that was missing that was filled when I had my pistol on me.

However, I could see my friends and family thought I was crazy. At the time I thought that may very well be true. Did I need a pistol to go get bread from the store?

Well, I believe the best answer is you aren't crazy at all. I'm not saying that every Combat Veteran needs to carry a gun. What I'm saying is if that makes you feel comfortable, then you should do so. You should do so knowing it comes from a completely stable train of thought.

You have seen the violence in the world. You have seen that there are some people who have no mercy or regard for human life.

When that person does decide that your life is worth the $37 in your pocket, or that your wife's wedding ring is more important than her breathing, you can defend yourself and your family.

That's a completely acceptable and rational train of thought to be able to protect yourself and your loved ones.

It doesn't make you crazy at all. You had two voices, one on each of your shoulders. The wrong one was telling you that you are crazy for carrying. Bitch smack that one and be done with it. Listen to the one that is right, the one that is telling you that you are a sheepdog. Hoping that there is no violence, but ready if it presents itself.

YOU ARE LOOKING AT AN AMERICAN

In nearly every VFW, you can hear Soldiers talk about the Gooks that they fought, or the Krauts or the Hajis.

In every war we have created some type of racial slur to identify our enemies. It's not politically correct, but it's true. That really shouldn't be shocking to many people, however, it is to some.

What would be surprising is to find out that we do it because we are good people.

Now your head would probably explode when hearing that. "How can a good person call another human being a racial slur?"

It's because we aren't designed to kill others.

We absolutely can, and will if necessary. At the end of the day, we basically only exist to do two primary functions:

survive and replicate. We want to stay alive and we want to make babies. There are very few exceptions to this rule. This is something we have done for thousands of years, it's a part of our DNA. Every action you do throughout the day, you can trace back to being attached to either your need to survive or to replicate.

Pressing a button to launch a missile to kill someone, is hard. Tossing a grenade into a room that you know has people in it is harder. Pulling the trigger on a silhouette that you see through your scope is harder. Firing a pistol round into someone's chest is even harder, yet slicing someone's throat with your knife is the hardest. Each one is more intimate and more personal.

We just simply aren't designed to kill. So how do you take an 18 year old kid and teach him or her to kill? You condition them. You don't have them shoot at targets on paper, you have them shoot a man-sized silhouette that pops up at certain times. You then psychologically reward them by having that target drop when it is hit. You further reward them with medals on their chest the better they shoot.

You condition them through singing cadences when they run.

"See that Taliban dressed in black, stab my bayonet in his back, see that Haji dressed in red, five five six round in his head. Who'll be alive when the morning comes? I don't know but I'll be one!"

There are a lot of different ways that military changes your mind to make it easier to kill. However, they can't change the fact that at the end of the day, you are going to have to kill another human being.

We make it so that we don't have to kill another guy who has a family at home. We don't have to kill a guy who probably likes cooking out and drinking beer on a warm Friday evening.

We kill Zipperheads, we kill Japs, we kill Camel Jockeys. They aren't us, they are scum.

It's a survival mechanism that we adapt. Whether or not it is necessary is up for debate, but what I want you to understand is that it served a certain purpose.

It served a certain purpose in a combat zone. However, you are no longer in a combat zone. You no longer have to kill. There are no Asians or Japanese or German people. There are only Americans. There are only people that came to this great country to get away from their country where they faced oppression or no economic opportunities. They saw the greatness that America offered and want to contribute. You can relate more than most people. You have seen the awful conditions they have lived in.

Now there are always going to be exceptions. There are always going to be people who come over here and just suck up government benefits, there will be terrorists who get through the security protocols. But there are also always going to be Americans that do the same. These people are the exceptions to the rule.

You aren't a bad person for de-humanizing your enemies. It was a survival mechanism that served its purpose.

However, you are back home now and you no longer need it.

ENJOY YOUR WORK

"Freedom is never more than one generation away from extinction. We didn't pass it to our children in the bloodstream. It must be fought for, protected, and handed on for them to do the same, or one day we will spend our sunset years telling our children and our children's children what it was once like in the United States where men were free." – Ronald Reagan

You are an elite individual. You have walked in the footsteps of the brave men and women that have fought so you could grow up with all of the liberties that you have enjoyed. You have then fought so the men and women who are now serving could do so with a memory of growing up under freedom.

Everybody that has ever worn the uniform is the reason you can step outside and yell "Politician Smith is a jackass!" without being imprisoned.

It's why you can openly practice your religion without being executed.

It's why you can be of whatever sexual orientation you wish and not be hung for it.

It's why women can be doctors and can drive cars.

You are the only reason all of these freedoms exist. YOU made that happen. So take some time to appreciate your work.

There are all kinds of beautiful moments that happen every day.

You see that cute elderly couple holding hands? Remember that YOU are the reason that they have been able to have all of those great years together.

You see those kids playing carelessly at the park? YOU are the reason they don't have to worry about a car bomb going off.

You have seen a side of this world that not many others have. You know that there are parts of the world where people live in pure terror every day. Where people live in poverty. Where people live in ignorance.

When you see something beautiful happen here in the states, take a second to just acknowledge your work. Take a second to understand just how powerful it is that YOU made it so that could happen.

I remember when I was doing distance running, I would always run past a park where there would be kids playing soccer, other kids would be on a swing set, a couple would be having a picnic on the grass, etc. It made my chest swell with pride that we live in such a beautiful country. I would then take a second to understand that sheepdogs like myself are the only reason this is possible.

It's not arrogance, it's not having a big head. It's understanding and accepting a FACT. That you are 100% the reason we live in such an amazing country.

THE MEDIA WANTS TO HELP

Chances are that the media isn't as bad or as corrupt as you think.

Well... at least when it comes to Veterans issues.

When I first got back, I HATED the media. They got it all wrong and they only interviewed politicians. They would interview some congressman who would talk about how he is doing this or that to help Veterans.

They had it all wrong.

I've been blessed to be on all kinds of different media - TV, newspaper, radio, you name it.

I can tell you that the grunts in the media industry are the reporter and the photographer (cameraman). They are the ones that do all of the hard work. It gets a bit more complicated when you get to national news, etc. But for the most part, when you see a reporter on the local news talking about a Veteran's issue, that reporter and his or her photog has free reign of the story. They've got to submit it for approval, but really it's up to them to report on it.

Wouldn't this reaffirm the fact that they are jacked up and don't tell the whole truth?

NO. In its most simplistic form, the way a news story happens is similar to below:

1. Editor tells the reporters what to report on in the morning. ("Go do a story on returning Veteran unemployment issues").
2. The reporter has to pull from their limited resources/ networks to get contacts, hoping they can find a Veteran to speak with.
3. The reporter interviews said contacts.
4. Reporters will take their unedited footage, go back to the office, edit it and put it together for a final product.
5. They get it approved.
6. It ends up on the evening news.

The breakdown is that most reporters don't have a lot of Veterans in their network. They put their feelers out in hopes that they can do justice, but while they may not have Veterans in their network, they definitely have a politician in their network. Instead of a true Veteran, they just interview the politician, thinking that they are getting reliable intel. However, those stories rarely tell the whole truth. That's why we end up with stories on the news that make most of us want to punch the TV screen.

That was an explanation, but complaining about something and not offering a solution really is just bitching. So I offer this solution:

REPORTERS WANT TO TALK TO COMBAT VETERANS. THEY WANT TO HEAR OUR STORIES.

The next time you see a politician on the news talking about "My office has spearheaded an initiative that will GUARANTEE that our returning Veterans will transition seamlessly back in to the civilian world", do the following:

Write down the reporters name if you see it on TV. If it is an internet article, they should have their name in the credit.

Reach out to them and offer your insight. Send them a message.

"Joe Reporter, I saw your news segment last night about how Congressman Johnson was talking about his great program to help returning Veterans. I don't think that you really have gotten the entire story. I have applied for that program and it has a 5 month waiting list. Furthermore, my friend Travis has just completed that training. It is just a one hour PowerPoint presentation where at the end they give you a pamphlet. It really isn't as effective as Congressman Johnson makes it out to be, and I'd love to talk with you more about not only that program, but about issues a lot of returning Veterans are facing."

Most of the reporters I know are our allies. These guys are ready to kick ass on our behalf. They just live their lives through rose colored glasses because they are unaware of what challenges we are facing.

I've never been burned by a reporter, not even once. They have all seemed to genuinely care about our issues and most seem legitimately pissed off when they find out about the struggles we have returning home.

So feel free to reach out to them, most of them are willing to give us a voice.

With that being said, if a politician has done something great for Veterans and are on TV talking about it, feel free to reach out to the reporter and tell them how they are spot on. How Congressman Smith leads the way and is bending over backwards to help us, etc.

THE REAL CHALLENGE

They say that ignorance is bliss. This is something I understand 100%. Before I started my organization, all I knew, was that nearly every person I talked to spoke of how they support our Veterans and how they would do anything to help us.

I then found out that there are basically four types of people in this world when it comes to supporting our Vets:

Group 1: These people are few and far between, but they exist. These are the people who think that we are baby killers or that we should die, etc. These guys are normally found trolling on online forums.

Group 2: People who just enjoy the novelty of being able to say "I support the troops" because they like to jump on the bandwagon. They will change their Facebook profile pictures on Veterans Day and will tell nearly anybody about how they support their troops because they once thanked a guy with a Veteran cap on. These are also the people who when they find out you are a Veteran will tell you that they basically know what it's like to serve because their cousin was in the Coast Guard. These are the people who will continue to preach that they stand behind our troops. That is until it's time to back it up. Until it's time to give a $5 donation to help a Veterans group. Until they have a Veteran in for a job interview and choose the other candidate because they don't want to have one of those "PTSD Veterans" working for them, etc.

Group 3: People who back up what they say. They donate when they can, they help at every opportunity that presents itself.

Group 4: I think this is the most common type of supporter. It's the person who really does support our Veterans but isn't sure how to best show it. They truly, in their heart, are appreciative and they stand for the National Anthem. Their hearts hurt when they hear about a Soldier that was killed in action. Their eyes tear up a little when they read an article about how 22 Veterans commit suicide every single day.

I have long said that the solution to taking care of our returning Veterans is to spread awareness and to change the policies that are in place that are failing our returning troops.

I think we have done a lot of work. We have came a long way since General Patton, who in 1943 slapped two Soldiers and called them "cowards", among other things for having PTSD. I mean, in less than 100 years we have made HUGE improvements. If we continue to advance just a little every day, we will soon be able to give our returning men and women the care they deserve.

The problem is that we are sometimes moving backwards. While I discuss some of the other areas where we are failing in other chapters of this book, I would be doing you a disservice if I didn't address possibly one of the biggest myths that exist about helping Veterans (at the time this book was written).

That the 22 pushup challenge is doing great things.

"Let's post a video of us doing 22 push-ups on video to represent the 22 Veterans we lose every day due to PTSD."

I think the majority of people who do this fall into Group 4. These are people who have been waiting for some way to show their support and then they see this opportunity and do it because they think it will make big changes. I say big changes, but these videos aren't making big changes at all. I would say they are tiny. I mean barely on the radar.

I think this also attracts a lot of people from Group 2. "Hey, I can do 22 push-ups (relatively easy) and then everybody will like my video and tell me how great of a supporter that I am."

Don't get me wrong, spreading awareness of the fact that we are losing 22 Veterans a day to suicide isn't bad. It's just nowhere near as powerful as everybody thinks that it is. This "Challenge" really isn't a challenge.

There really isn't any skin in the game to do this because it isn't hard. You don't have to leave your house, you can do it in less than 5 minutes and you are psychologically rewarded by the praise you get from it.

I know there are going to be a lot of people that disagree and that's fine, but what I would like to present to you is a challenge that you may not get a lot of praise for (if any) It will cost you time and possibly some money and it will probably be stepping outside of your comfort zone. But it's a solution, it's something that will really make a difference.

I challenge you to do something once a month that shows your appreciation to our Veterans.

Donate $10 to a Veteran organization of your choice.

That old World War II Veteran who lives on the corner, shovel his sidewalk and driveway the next time it snows.

Bake some cookies or a pie for a Veteran you may know.

If you are a hiring manager, give preference to an applicant if they are a Veteran.

Gift a Veteran this book.

The next time you see that Veteran who lives down the road from you who flies that Navy flag out on his porch, stop by and get to know him a little better. Ask him to tell you some stories of his time in service.

Make a handmade gift for a Veteran that you know.

These are just a couple of examples, you can use your imagination but do something that is more personable than just making a quick video.

You may think when you are reading these ideas that you will be doing THEM a great service, but you will be surprised how rewarding this will be for you as well.

This is where real change will happen. It will happen by the individuals that decide to stand up and make a difference. If you accept this challenge, I salute you.

SHOW GRATITUDE EVERY DAY

Practicing gratitude every day is a great way to change your outlook on life. I know it seems like a hippy practice where you walk around in a hemp shirt and go up to a flower and whisper "I appreciate you", but being thankful for things that you have in your life will dramatically improve your mood.

When I first got out of the military, I was not a happy person and I wasn't thankful for much at all. It's easy to get stuck in a rut, but the truth is that there is always SOMETHING to be thankful for. It reminds me of an old saying "I complained that I had no shoes, until I met a man with no feet."

You have a TON of things to be thankful for, whether you know it or not. Did you know that almost half of the world lives on less than $2.50 per day? You might have spent that much on your coffee this morning.

But even if you didn't know that, you do have real world experience. For me, I sometimes still fall into a rut. When

I do, I think back to the Iraqis that would beg for food or the ones that would have to hide their bibles in their houses because they would be executed if someone found out they were not Muslim.

It's all about perspective, but chances are that if you are reading this, you are not in a country where you have to worry about roadside bombs going off or if today you will starve to death. So by default, if you don't have to worry about those things, then you have an incredible amount to be grateful for.

Start by writing a list. Get a piece of paper and write down 20 things that you are thankful for, it could be anything from your family, your car, your job, your friends, to your family, your pet, etc. It doesn't matter how trivial it is, just start writing down things that you are thankful for. Maybe you are thankful for having the eyesight to read this book.

Chances are that when you do it, you will feel joyful. It will actually make you feel better.

It's impossible to feel both sad and happy at the same time.

Now let's continue doing that on a daily basis. There are a ton of different ways to practice gratitude. Some people actually keep a gratitude journal. Every night before bedtime, they will write down three things they are grateful for. This can also help you with your sleep because you are putting positive thoughts into your head before you fall asleep and dream.

In the beginning, I did the journal but it was hit or miss and sometimes I would forget. So what I did was I set three different alarms on my phone. One at 1100, one at 1600 and one at 2000. Then when the alarm went off I would say to myself "I am so incredibly thankful that..."

If that works for you, then use it. Perhaps you have an idea of a reminder that might work better for you. Perhaps it is saying something you are thankful for before you eat, maybe it's before you go to work, after work, before bed, etc.

The thing is that you just need to understand that life is beautiful and there are wonderful things all around us.

Also, if you are wondering, I now say at least three things that I am grateful for before I go to bed at night. I also have it set up so that whenever someone purchases one of my books, a notification gets sent to my phone and when it does, I stop whatever I am doing and give thanks right then and there.

It's not about the money, I'm thankful that I found my gift and that I am able to use it to make this world a better place. That I am able to help my brothers and sisters live a healthier, happier life.

Thank you for purchasing this book and reminding me that I have so much to be thankful about in this beautiful world.

START AN EXERCISE PROGRAM

Whether or not you have PTSD, regular exercise has a number of benefits.

I know my thought process when I got out of the service was "I don't have to exercise anymore, the only way I'm running ANYWHERE is if the zombie apocalypse happens".

When we were in the service, we exercised every day and it was just something that we did. We didn't really understand the true benefits of it. It's obvious the physical benefits that we get out of it, but there are a ton of psychological benefits, too.

Exercise releases endorphins into the brain. These are drugs that make you feel happy. You may have heard of "runners high", well that's exactly what I'm referring to.

While everything in this book is something that I had to learn the hard way because there wasn't any information on it at the time, I wish I would have learned this first as the benefits are amazing.

I started exercising by accident. At the time, I was running an organization to help Veterans. A guy came to me and wanted to start a Jiu-Jitsu program. This pretty much made sense to me because ground fighting fell right in line with Army Combatives. We started the program, and it was a success. It actually worked out really well. We would jokingly talk trash about each other and then put three minutes on the clock and wouldn't stop until one of us tapped or passed out from a choke. We were covered in sweat by the end of the day, but we always felt great.

Eventually, I decided I wanted to continue exercising and start running on my own.

Actually, let me back track. If you were in the military, you know that it sucks all the fun out of anything you could possibly get enjoyment out of.

You like shooting guns? Not with a ton of Range Safety's yelling through a bullhorn.

You like to rappel? Not when the instructors have to barnify everything and put so many safety precautions on things that it's no longer enjoyable.

You like to run? Well not when you're in between run groups and you either have one that you can't keep up with, or the opposite, where you are in one that is slowed down to the point where you might as well be walking.

When I was in, I HATED running. I mean I hated everything about it, but with the new Jiu-Jitsu program, I wanted to be able to keep my cardio up because I was tired of Gilbert (your stereotypical infantry shit-talking Marine) talking smack.

So I started running again. But it's different when you aren't in the military. I actually began to enjoy it. If I wanted to sprint up a hill and run until I puked, I could. If I wanted to just go for a jog for a couple of miles along the river, I could do that too. I could just throw on my IPod and get lost in the nature.

It's amazing how something I hated so much is now something I enjoy with a passion.

That's the power of exercising, it becomes addictive because you feel good not only physically, but mentally as well. Exercise is a NATURAL anti-depressant.

So start exercising as soon as possible. The trick is to find something that you enjoy. Exercising comes in various forms:

Biking

Running

Walking

Weight-lifting

Yoga

Jiu-Jitsu

Crossfit

Rock climbing

Dancing

Skating

Paintball

Sports (basketball, baseball, etc.)

As you can see, exercise comes in many different forms. Find one that you are attracted to and start doing it a minimum of twice weekly.

Many of the things I talk about in this book can be coupled. This could be one as well. You could use this as an opportunity to branch out and meet new people. You could join a running group, or a yoga studio, etc.

Me personally, this is my time to myself. I hit the trail, and it's just me and my music. I'll run a couple of hours and feel completely recharged at the end.

POLITICIANS

While this book is geared to help my brothers and sisters, I would like to dedicate this chapter to those who are hindering the process of helping our returning Veterans.

To the politicians that are all talk.

It may seem shocking that I have written a chapter on this, but I would be doing both myself and my brothers and sisters a disservice if I were not to mention it.

If you are a Veteran reading this book, then chances are you already understand. If you are a civilian, or perhaps even a Veteran that hasn't been enlightened yet, then know that most politicians are snakes.

They are vultures that look for a Veteran to run up to, snap a photo with and then tell their voters about how much they care about "The heroic Men and Women who sacrifice so much for this great Nation", or some other recited verse that they think will get votes.

This isn't speculation either. My first book LITERALLY started out as a letter to the President. I sent that version of it to about every politician I could think of with NO reply at all. No email response, no snail mail response, NOTHING.

But once I got pissed off, I took that original letter and turned it into a book. My, how things have changed. When my first book came out, I made the front page of the local newspaper and my phone rang off the hook with politicians wanting to "talk" to me.

It's funny how nobody listened to Specialist Hutchison, nobody listened to Daniel Hutchison the Veteran. But holy crap, once I had a platform to stand on they flocked to me. I figured that I had finally made it. That now I can talk directly to the decision makers and we can make some change. Sadly, that was short-lived as well. It was more of "Hey, let's get a picture together" and less of talking about how we can work together to take care of our returning Veterans.

Hell, I once met Vice President Biden. I definitely thought I was onto something there! We had a meeting arranged once he was done with a speech he was giving at a city close to me. We spoke briefly, he then told me he was in a hurry but to contact him and we could talk (after he got a picture of course). I spent weeks afterwards emailing and calling, but nothing. This was one of the most powerful men in the country. One that I thought would listen to me so we could work together to make a change. But he was just another politician with empty promises.

That was surprising to me as his son had served in Iraq. Well, I guess it was surprising at the time. I guess when you step back and look at it, it's unlikely that the Son of the Vice President of The United States of America would deal with long wait times at the VA or delayed treatment, or lost records, etc.

With that being said, I do need to give credit where credit is due. I once met with Senator Sherrod Brown. He invited me to Washington and met with me over coffee. I stayed in touch with his office. At the time, I ran an organization that helped Veterans transition back to civilian life. I can tell you one thing – If I got to a point where I needed someone to step in on a VA claim to help a Vet, or one of my brothers or sisters were being mistreated by the VA, I knew with confidence that I could call his office and it would be handled QUICKLY. Now those actions were done by his staff, not him. But as anyone in the military knows, the lowest ranking private is a reflection of the Sergeant Major and how he runs his unit.

That is me giving credit where credit is due. This isn't political. In fact, I disagree with a lot of his policies. But he was an ass kicker when asses needed to be kicked for Veterans in need.

If you are a politician out there, saying that you are doing something and not doing it is worse than doing nothing at all. Don't light a fire in a Veteran and tell them that you are going to help them, we look up to you. For the most part, we are powerless. We can't demand to speak with a manager at the VA. We can't fire our healthcare provider at the VA and go to a different hospital. Our hands are tied.

Here is my challenge to any and ALL politicians out there. Once a month, have lunch with a Veteran and just listen to them. Listen to their stories. Listen to how things really are for them. THAT is how you are going to make a change. That is what will allow you to have insight when you vote on bills that affect how they are taken care of. THAT is how you will be able to look into the camera with an incredible amount of confidence and say "I don't just talk the talk, I walk the walk. I care about the men and women who have sacrificed so much for this great country."

ONE ACT OF KINDNESS

Do something nice for others and do it at least once a day.

When I first got back, "nice" was definitely not a word that most people would use to describe me. I was angry at the world, and that definitely showed.

I then attended a seminar and during our lunch break they said to go do something nice for someone. It actually kind of made me freeze up. "What the hell am I going to do to be nice to someone? I don't even like people."

So I drove to lunch and parked my car and put some change in the meter. While I was walking from my car to the restaurant, I saw a meter that was expired but had a car parked in the spot, and there wasn't a ticket on the windshield. SCORE, I thought to myself! I can just put a quarter in here and I'd have done my good deed and I don't even have to talk to someone. So I put some change in and almost as soon as

I did, I heard someone yell "HEY!", then they started to approach me.

"Is this guy looking for a fight?" I asked myself.

"Hey, I was running out to put more change in, please don't give me a ticket".

He thought I was a cop writing him a ticket. Once he got closer, I told him that I was just putting in some change to be nice. This guy's eyes started watering and he told me that he was in a job interview and that he had been out of work for a while. That he literally only had a couple of bucks to his name so he tried to gauge the length of the interview appropriately because at the point, even an extra quarter was big deal to him.

I was actually kind of touched by the story and my heart swelled with pride, but at that time I wasn't sure how to show emotion and it scared me so I just said "It's just something I had to do, don't mention it." I then walked off.

After lunch, I went back to the seminar, they finished the lecture, and told us that every day you should do something nice for someone else. They then asked the audience what they had done during the lunch break.

"I paid for the car behind mine's meal." Said one person.

"I held the door open for someone at the store." Said another.

"I complimented the cashier at the gas station about her hair." Said another.

They told of all the things that they had done and how it made them feel.

This is a powerful exercise that I still do today. Every day I do at least one kind act. Sometimes it's little things like opening doors for people. Sometimes it's big things like stopping on the side of the road and helping someone change a tire. There are a ton of nice things you can do:

Compliment someone

Smile at somebody

Hold a door open for someone

Stop and help someone on the side of the road

Stop by and check on one of your elderly neighbors

Bring your co-worker their favorite cup of coffee

Put some coins in someone's parking meter so they don't get a ticket.

Give a bigger than usual tip

Pick up some litter you see on the ground.

Write someone a letter letting them know you appreciate them.

This is just a handful of suggestions. There are a ton of ways you can do something to brighten someone's day and the more you do it, the easier it gets. Before you know it, you will be doing it automatically.

This isn't just to help them, either. You would be surprised at how great it makes you feel!

Approximately a month ago, I was at a seminar, and during a break, I was in the bathroom washing my hands. The janitor walked in and looked grumpy, like he hated his job. He was slumped over his cleaning cart. Before I left, I told him that I appreciate how clean and great the bathrooms look and thanked him. He went from that grumpy look to a beaming smile and his whole posture changed. I'm sure that I changed his mood and maybe even his day! It didn't cost me anything!

Start doing one nice thing a day and you will be surprised at how it changes the way you feel!

LEARN TO COOK

This is therapeutic and I can't stress this enough. When I first got back from Iraq, I was a single Soldier so my life consisted of value menu dinners and TV dinners… and a lot of whiskey.

One day I was on the internet and someone shared a recipe that looked amazing. I mean it looked really good, and at first I got depressed thinking that I didn't know how to cook and there was nobody to cook it for me. Then the thought popped into my head "Hey, you could cook it yourself", but I had absolutely NO idea how to cook anything so I pretty much just gave up on the idea.

Then the SAME recipe was shared again about a week later. So I ended up opening the link and there were only a couple of ingredients, and really the instructions didn't look too complicated. I figured "What the hell, if you jack it up you can just throw it away and you'll only be out a couple bucks".

So I went and bought the ingredients and began cooking. WOW, there is something about cooking that is just on another level if you have never tried it before. I know there are tons of studies that prove that having a hobby where you work with your hands is good for people with PTSD, but I never would have guessed that cooking would have helped the way that it did.

I mean it was enjoyable right from the moment I got all of the ingredients out and started chopping them up, measuring, etc.

Cooking demands your attention. It doesn't let you be anywhere else at the moment. You are right there chopping and mixing. It doesn't allow your brain to wander off.

Then, once you finish cooking and you have a final product. It is SUCH a sense of accomplishment.

You aren't always going to hit it big with cooking. There have been plenty of times that I have cooked some things that I had to force myself to eat, but those are few and far between. It's like any other skill, the more you do it, the better you will get at it.

There are a TON of different recipe websites out there, so just do a Google search and you will find one that interests you.

If you have a family, you will see that it saves you a lot of money from eating out. If you are single then you may try to justify the cost, but you will actually save money. Most recipes are designed to feed more than one person, so you will have leftovers. Go buy a Tupperware container and when you are finished cooking, you'll have your lunch for the next day. If you do the math, you will see that you are cooking two meals, saving yourself money and tomorrow at lunch time you just have to pop your lunch in the microwave.

You can choose to cook healthy or not. Really it doesn't matter, just get out there and start doing it.

You could combine this with another lesson learned. Invite someone over you'd like to date and cook for them. You could also invite your friends over and show off your skills. Another idea would be to invite someone over that you've kind of distanced yourself from, and cook a meal for them. This could be a baby step or a small way of opening a door to get back into a relationship with them. You could also have the honor or being taught how to cook by someone that you love. Maybe you've always wanted to learn how to cook that meatloaf your mom makes, or maybe your grandma makes amazing lasagna. Think of how thrilled they would be if you asked them to teach you how to cook.

Try it for yourself, do me that favor. Hell, do YOURSELF that favor. You won't regret it.

YOUR JOB WAS MISSION ESSENTIAL

"It's the Special Forces Soldier that is really fighting the fight."

"It's the Marines that are kicking down doors and getting high value targets that are really making a difference."

"My job wasn't very important."

That's something I hear a lot of Veterans who weren't in a combat MOS say.

Hollywood has glamorized the Soldier with a bandana wrapped around his head, holding an M-16 in each hand with a 100% hit rate while smoking a cigarette as model Veteran. Just as society has modeled a size 0 waist as the perfect female.

The problem is that ideology is damaging to both examples.

I'm not taking anything away from the Infantry or Special Operations community. They have definitely earned their right to be called a "bad ass".

What I'm saying is that just because you DIDN'T do all of that stuff, it doesn't mean you were insignificant.

I would like to share with you a story about leadership that I learned in Baghdad:

In Iraq, I was one of only 4 medics on a small base that was used to stage the door kickers during the troop surge. If they ran over a road side bomb or kicked down a door and a bad guy shot first, they would come to us for treatment. We were over-worked and understaffed. But, I had the best damn squad in the U.S. Army and my NCO's would always cover for us and send us to get some hot chow during lunch. However, once the surge started picking up, I started to get paranoid, our radios that we kept on us were not always reliable and I would always be scared that I would not be at the Aid Station when incoming casualties arrived. Also, most of the time my nerves were shot, and I couldn't eat anyways. When my Staff Sergeant relieved me for chow, I'd just run to the chow hall, get a coffee and run back, I'd then spend 10 minutes (so Staff Sergeant thought I ate) or so smoking and hanging out within eyesight of the Aid Station so that if casualties came in I would be able to see it and help. I'd either do that or if I was able to eat, I'd get a hotbox and bring it back to the Aid Station to eat.

Well, there was one day where I just wanted to sit down and eat in the chow hall. I was tired and just wanted to enjoy my meal. I got my food and looked around. We were a SMALL base before the surge, so when the additional troops came in, it really took it's toll on our base. There was only one table with seats open. I moved closer and could see it was full of higher ranking Soldiers than myself. I moved even closer and started to see their 82nd Airborne patches and Ranger tabs. "Man, I'm going to sit here and they are going to eat me alive. These are America's best and I'm just a National Guard Medic."

I sat down and they actually engaged me in conversation. I was surprised, I mean these guys were the elite, but they didn't act like they were better than me. They talked to me like we were equals. I did the common courtesies of saying "Yes Sergeant, No Sergeant, etc." Eventually one of the Staff Sergeants said "Look fucker, quit addressing me as Sergeant and eye-ball fucking my tab. This surge is a shit-storm and at any point we can all be equals. Tomorrow I may have a hole in my neck and be looking at you to save me. Over here it's one team, one fight. We can save that hierarchy shit for when we get back to the states."

I will always remember that day as one of the most significant lessons in my military career. It taught me that the military is a machine. Every Soldier is a cog in it, an important piece. One may be more glamourous than the other, one may have a harder title to earn, but none are more important than the other.

You may have had your own personal vehicle completely stop working over a small, $10 part before. That's because it's just as important as the larger parts. If that quits working, the whole system fails. Well, the military is the same way.

Your job as supply is important because if it weren't for you, the mechanic couldn't get the wrench that is needed to fix the HMMWV to transport the troops.

Your job as signal is important because if you didn't get the antenna up, the medevac couldn't be heard when it was called in.

Your job as an engineer is important because if you didn't construct that helipad, the Apache couldn't come in and refuel/resupply and provide the air support that the ground troops needed.

Everything works together, it's all part of a bigger plan.

If you were in a postal unit, the ground troops morale was kept high because you made sure their letters from home got to them.

If you were in a finance unit, you made sure their pay was squared away so they didn't have to worry about bills while they were over there.

Never discredit yourself or downplay what you did over there.

THE BEST YEARS OF YOUR LIFE

Did you waste the "best years of your life" while you were serving your country?

The answer is yes for some people.

The answer is no for some people.

The correct answer is only if you believe that the best years of your life are gone.

When I was over there, I jokingly but not jokingly talked to a Captain about how I was spending the best years of my life in combat while my friends were all graduating college and starting families. He gave me some sound advice.

"Life is like a book. It's a series of chapters. Some chapters are going to end, so just come to terms with that. But there will be trade offs. There was a chapter when you were young, but you may have been broke. There might be a chapter where you aren't a teenager anymore, but you also don't make dumb decisions as often, etc. But you are constantly writing your book. So the best years of your life? That's today. That's tomorrow. Write a book that you will be proud of."

My struggles with PTSD were some of the darkest chapters of my life. They were some of my loneliest. Some of the most embarrassing. But I can now understand that they were chapters. That page has turned. I am now writing my own book. Every day I get to wake up with a fresh page, a new canvas. I get to create the best days of my life.

Your tour in combat was a very important chapter of your life, but it was just that. It was a chapter that is in the past. Throughout this book, I hope you find tools that will help you understand how to write a book that is filled with love, laughter and joy.

HELP ME CREATE HISTORY

"It's the action, not the fruit of the action, that's important. You have to do the right thing. It may not be in your power, may not be in your time, that there'll be any fruit. But that doesn't mean you stop doing the right thing. You may never know what results come from your action. But if you do nothing, there will be no result."
- Mahatma Gandhi

We are currently fighting a battle that we have never had before.

There was once a time when if you got injured while fighting in the Civil War, it was nearly a guarantee that you would lose a limb or die from infection, because there was little understanding of how infection worked.

There was once a time where if you got an ailment, the doctor would perform a technique called "Bloodletting" where they would literally cut you and let you bleed out a certain amount of blood, because at that time, they believed that cured you.

We now look back on those times, and it seems so silly. With the knowledge we have today, it almost seems unreal that those events could have happened.

I firmly believe that 100 years from now, our children and grandchildren will say

"There was once a time when 22 Veterans committed suicide every day because we didn't understand PTSD or how to break down the stigma surrounding it."

"There was once a time when returning Veterans got little to no help transitioning back to civilian life. They were just left on their own."

I believe they will say those things ONLY if you have the courage to fight with me. Only if you have the courage to stand by my side as we fight together to take care of our returning brothers and sisters.

I just want to reiterate how big this is – Since the beginning of time, we have had war and we have continually tried to figure out ways to make a human being better at killing. We have made technological advances in weaponry, but we have also committed so many resources to change our warrior's minds. "How can we change their mindset so that they can kill another human being?" The investment in that continues up until they are discharged from the military. They are then given a pat on the back, their discharge papers, and are shown the door. There isn't much training to teach them how to become a civilian again.

We have the power to do something that has never before been done in history.

I know this book isn't a cure all, but I stand confident that it is a huge step in the right direction. Everything in this book is what has taken me from a point where I was suicidal to who I am now. Furthermore, these are also tips and techniques that I have used to help hundreds of my brothers and sisters live a happy, healthy life.

One person can make a difference. I ask you to stand with me and help get OUR message out to the world. Keep this book so you can always have it as a reference, but gift one to another Veteran. By doing so, you will likely improve the quality of their life and you very well may save their life.

Gift one to your friend that you served with.

Gift one to the Vietnam Veteran that lives down the road.

If you don't know of any Veterans around you, donate one to your local VFW or AMVETS. They will know how to make sure it gets in the right hands.

I'm not asking you to buy multiple books, just one more to help spread this powerful message.

One person can make a difference. One act of kindness can change a life.

There was once a time when my foolish pride wouldn't have allowed me to ask you to do that, but that's how confident I am about the contents of this book and the power they have. I know it can change lives.

Together, we can make a huge difference in this world. One book at a time. One person at a time.

CPSIA information can be obtained
at www.ICGtesting.com
Printed in the USA
FFOW05n1515160117